MW01289692

TPM Simplified

By Ade Asefeso MCIPS MBA

First Edition

ISBN-13: 978-1500596804

ISBN-10: 1500596809

Publisher: AA Global Sourcing Ltd
Website: http://www.aaglobalsourcing.com

Table of Contents

Disclaimer

This publication is designed to provide competent and reliable information regarding the subject matter covered. However, it is sold with the understanding that the author and publisher are not engaged in rendering professional advice. The authors and publishers specifically disclaim any liability that is incurred from the use or application of contents of this book.

If you purchased this book without a cover you should be aware that this book may have been stolen property and reported as "unsold and destroyed" to the publisher. In this case neither the author nor the publisher has received any payment for this "stripped book."

Dedication

To my family and friends who seems to have been sent here to teach me something about who I am supposed to be. They have nurtured me, challenged me, and even opposed me.... But at every juncture has taught me!

This book is dedicated to my lovely boys, Thomas, Michael and Karl. Teaching them to manage their finance will give them the lives they deserve. They have taught me more about life, presence, and energy management than anything I have done in my life.

Chapter 1: Introduction

What is Total Productive Maintenance (TPM) ?

It can be considered as the medical science of machines. Total Productive Maintenance (TPM) is a maintenance program which involves a defined concept for maintaining plants and equipment. The goal of the TPM program is to markedly increase production while, at the same time, increasing employee moral and job satisfaction.

TPM brings maintenance into focus as a necessary and vitally important part of the business. It is no longer regarded as a non-profit activity. Down time for maintenance is scheduled as part of the manufacturing day and, in some cases, as an integral part of the manufacturing process. The goal is to hold emergency and unscheduled maintenance to a minimum.

Why TPM ?

TPM was introduced to achieve the following objectives. The important ones are listed below.

1. Avoid wastage in a quickly changing economic environment.
2. Producing goods without reducing product quality.
3. Reduce cost.
4. Produce a low batch quantity at the earliest possible time.

5. Goods send to the customers must be non defective.

Similarities and differences between TQM and TPM:

The TPM program closely resembles the popular Total Quality Management (TQM) program. Many of the tools such as employee empowerment, benchmarking, documentation, etc. used in TQM are used to implement and optimize TPM. The following are the similarities between the two.

1. Total commitment to the program by upper level management is required in both programmes.
2. Employees must be empowered to initiate corrective action.
3. A long range outlook must be accepted as TPM may take a year or more to implement and is an on-going process. Changes in employee mind-set toward their job responsibilities must take place as well.

The differences between TQM and TPM is summarized below.

Types of maintenance

1. Breakdown maintenance

It means that people waits until equipment fails and repair it. Such a thing could be used when the equipment failure does not significantly affect the operation or production or generate any significant loss other than repair cost.

2. Preventive maintenance

It is a daily maintenance (cleaning, inspection, oiling and re-tightening), design to retain the healthy condition of equipment and prevent failure through the prevention of deterioration, periodic inspection or equipment condition diagnosis, to measure deterioration. It is further divided into periodic maintenance and predictive maintenance. Just like human life is extended by preventive medicine, the equipment service life can be prolonged by doing preventive maintenance.

2a. Periodic maintenance (Time based maintenance - TBM):

Time based maintenance consists of periodically inspecting, servicing and cleaning equipment and replacing parts to prevent sudden failure and process problems.

2b. Predictive maintenance:

This is a method in which the service life of important part is predicted based on inspection or diagnosis, in order to use the parts to the limit of their service life. Compared to periodic maintenance, predictive maintenance is condition based maintenance. It manages trend values, by measuring and analyzing data about deterioration and employs a surveillance system, designed to monitor conditions through an on-line system.

3. Corrective maintenance

It improves equipment and its components so that preventive maintenance can be carried out reliably. Equipment with design weakness must be redesigned to improve reliability or improving maintainability.

4. Maintenance prevention

It indicates the design of a new equipment. Weakness of current machines are sufficiently studied (on site information leading to failure prevention, easier maintenance and prevents of defects, safety and ease of manufacturing) and are incorporated before commissioning a new equipment.

Chapter 2: The History of TPM

TPM is a innovative Japanese concept. The origin of TPM can be traced back to 1951 when preventive maintenance was introduced in Japan; however the concept of preventive maintenance was taken from USA. Nippon Denso was the first company to introduce plant wide preventive maintenance in 1960.

Preventive maintenance is the concept wherein, operators produced goods using machines and the maintenance group was dedicated with work of maintaining those machines, however with the automation of Nippon Denso, maintenance became a problem as more maintenance personnel were required. So the management decided that the routine maintenance of equipment would be carried out by the operators. (This is Autonomous maintenance, one of the features of TPM). Maintenance group took up only essential maintenance works.

Thus Nippon Denso which already followed preventive maintenance also added Autonomous maintenance done by production operators. The maintenance crew went in the equipment modification for improving reliability. The modifications were made or incorporated in new equipment. This lead to maintenance prevention. Thus preventive maintenance along with Maintenance prevention and Maintainability Improvement gave birth to Productive maintenance. The aim of productive maintenance was to maximize plant and equipment effectiveness to achieve optimum life cycle cost of production equipment.

By then Nippon Denso had made quality circles, involving the employees participation. Thus all employees took part in implementing Productive maintenance. Based on these developments Nippon Denso was awarded the distinguished plant prize for developing and implementing TPM, by the Japanese Institute of Plant Engineers (JIPE). Thus Nippon Denso of the Toyota group became the first company to obtain the TPM certification.

TPM Targets

1. Obtain Minimum 80% OPE.
2. Obtain Minimum 90% OEE (Overall Equipment Effectiveness)
3. Run the machines even during lunch. (Lunch is for operators and not for machines!)
4. Operate in a manner, so that there are no customer complaints.
5. Reduce the manufacturing cost by 30%.
6. Achieve 100% success in delivering the goods as required by the customer.
7. Maintain a accident free environment.
8. Increase the suggestions by 3 times. Develop Multi-skilled and flexible workers.

Motives of TPM

1. Adoption of life cycle approach for improving the overall performance of production equipment.

2. Improving productivity by highly motivated workers which is achieved by job enlargement.
3. The use of voluntary small group activities for identifying the cause of failure, possible plant and equipment modifications.

Uniqueness of TPM

The major difference between TPM and other concepts is that the operators are also made involve in the maintenance process. The concept of "I (Production operators) Operate, You (Maintenance department) fix" is not followed.

TPM Objectives

1. Achieve Zero Defects, Zero Breakdown and Zero accidents in all functional areas of the organization.
2. Involve people in all levels of organization.
3. Form different teams to reduce defects and Self Maintenance.

Direct benefits of TPM

1. Increase productivity and OPE (Overall Plant Efficiency) by 1.5 or 2 times.
2. Rectify customer complaints.
3. Reduce the manufacturing cost by 30%.
4. Satisfy the customer's needs by 100% (Delivering the right quantity at the right time, in the required quality.)
5. Reduce accidents.

6. Follow pollution control measures.

Indirect benefits of TPM

1. Higher confidence level among the employees.
2. Keep the work place clean, neat and attractive.
3. Favourable change in the attitude of the operators.
4. Achieve goals by working as team.
5. Horizontal deployment of a new concept in all areas of the organization.
6. Share knowledge and experience.
7. The workers get a feeling of owning the machine.

Overall Equipment Efficiency (OEE)

$OEE = A \times PE \times Q$

A - Availability of the machine. Availability is proportion of time machine is actually available out of time it should be available.

$A = (MTBF - MTTR)/MTBF.$

MTBF - Mean Time Between Failures = (Total Running Time)/Number of Failures.

MTTR - Mean Time To Repair.

PE - Performance Efficiency. It is given by RE X SE.

Rate efficiency (RE): Actual average cycle time is slower than design cycle time because of jams, etc. Output is reduced because of jams

Speed efficiency (SE): Actual cycle time is slower than design cycle time machine output is reduced because it is running at reduced speed.

Q - Refers to quality rate. Which is percentage of good parts out of total produced sometimes called "yield".

Chapter 3: Autonomous Maintenance

What is Autonomous Maintenance?

Autonomous maintenance is "independent" maintenance carried out by the operators of the machines rather than by dedicated maintenance technicians. This is core concept of TPM or Total productive maintenance, much like TQM (total quality management), TPM gives more responsibility and authority to the operators and releases the technical personnel to do more preventative and improvement works.

Unlike traditional maintenance programs where the operators run the machines until they break or become due for maintenance and then hand them to the maintenance department, autonomous maintenance has the operators performing the simpler (and safe) maintenance routines such as lubrication, bolt tightening, cleaning and also inspection and monitoring.

As the people that have day to day contact with the machines they are the most familiar with the operation of each machine and with full training can come to understand the functioning of the equipment. This enables them to feel greater ownership for their work and become more in control of how things are done and what improvements are made.

A role shift can blend operations and maintenance into a cohesive team.

At the core of world-class maintenance performance is something called autonomous maintenance. In this context, the term autonomous doesn't mean performing maintenance in a vacuum or solely by the traditional maintenance department. Rather, it means that operators perform certain equipment maintenance activities and that maintenance crafts get closely involved in the daily operation of equipment. The focus of the operating team is on cleaning, inspecting, lubricating, monitoring and other such essential daily tasks traditionally within the domain of the maintenance department.

Unfortunately, most equipment operators lack a feeling of ownership. The conventional philosophy in many underperforming plants is "I run it, you fix it," or "I'm manufacturing, you're maintenance." The older the company, the more rooted this mind-set becomes and the more difficult it is to change. In world-class plants, the operator becomes the asset owner, the focus for routine maintenance and the central figure in overall equipment effectiveness.

Real operator involvement

Operators can make or break maintenance effectiveness. Without interrupting their production work, operators can easily prevent breakdowns, predict failures and prolong equipment life if they become more intimately familiar with the machinery they run every day. But to do this, they must become highly equipment-conscious, and that can require some intense training. For example, operators must know what constitutes normal and abnormal operation. They need to know what they should listen for and be alert to. They must know what to do to keep machines in normal operating condition; lubricating them regularly, monitoring vital signs and recording abnormalities. They must also know what to do to get the machine back online when something goes wrong; fix minor problem, call maintenance for major problems and to schedule repairs. These actions are not intuitive for equipment operators; they must be learned.

Also, operators must be taught how, when and what to lubricate, as well as the best methods for checking lubrication. If operators aren't in the habit of cleaning their equipment, which, in world-class organizations, also means inspecting, operators will need to learn. Keeping debris from around machinery and other simple, good housekeeping is not necessarily part of the conventional operator's job description, but it's mandatory for achieving maintenance excellence.

Through formal classroom and on-the-job training, operators will learn what to look for during those inspections. They will begin to see equipment from a maintenance viewpoint as well as from an operator's perspective. They will learn their machines' critical points, areas of greatest wear potential and the relationships between operational abnormalities and root causes.

In the course of becoming more equipment-savvy, a sense of ownership will begin to take hold. With ownership comes an understanding of the role the equipment plays in producing quality output and how this new operator/machine relationship fits with the goals of the company. A new confidence in being able to diagnose problems accurately and devise solutions confidently will emerge. Operators become more creative problem solvers as they become more comfortable in the new, empowered role.

Autonomous benefits

Every company has invested heavily in developing the maintenance skills required to troubleshoot, repair and rebuild critical assets that comprise the facility. In most cases, each maintenance technician has received tens, if not hundreds, of thousands of dollars worth of formal and practical on-the-job training. Therefore, it seems illogical to waste this investment by having the best maintenance technicians in the house perform low-skill activities, such as inspections, lubrication, calibration and minor adjustments.

Involving operators in routine care and maintenance of critical plant assets offers three major benefits. The most obvious is reduced maintenance labour cost. In addition, the proximity of the operator to the asset greatly reduces or eliminates travel time, waiting for availability and other inefficiencies. Overall, autonomous maintenance represents a much better use of resources.

The second advantage is an increase in the availability of the highly skilled maintenance workforce for those maintenance activities that require greater specialized talents.

In most cases, serious maintenance activities, such as rebuilds and overhauls, can be performed much more effectively and efficiently under autonomous maintenance. This is especially important for offsetting the drastic population reduction in the skilled maintenance workforce during the past decade. An inadequately staffed workforce isn't a good excuse for avoiding or ignoring critical maintenance tasks.

The third benefit is the elimination of the "we-they" syndrome so prevalent in many plants. To be truly world-class, maintenance and production must function as an integrated team. Involving the operators in routine care and maintenance of the plant's assets will begin to crumble the traditional barriers between these two departments.

The ultimate reason for autonomous maintenance is simply that it saves money and improves bottom-line profitability. Operators are typically under used and have the time to perform these lower-skilled tasks. Transferring these tasks to operating teams improves the payback on the burdened, sunk cost of the production workforce and, at the same time, permits more effective use of the maintenance crafts.

Chapter 4: TPM Stages

STAGE A - Preparatory Stage

STEP 1 - Announcement by Management to all about TPM introduction in the organization:

Proper understanding, commitment and active involvement of the top management in needed for this step. Senior management should have awareness programmes, after which announcement is made to all. Publish it in the house magazine and put it in the notice board. Send a letter to all concerned individuals if required.

STEP 2 - Initial education and propaganda for TPM:

Training is to be done based on the need. Some need intensive training and some just an awareness. Take people who matters to places where TPM is already successfully implemented.

STEP 3 - Setting up TPM and departmental committees:

TPM includes improvement, autonomous maintenance, quality maintenance etc., as part of it. When committees are set up it should take care of all of those needs.

STEP 4 - Establishing the TPM working system and target:

Now each area is benchmarked and fix up a target for achievement.

STEP 5 - A master plan for institutionalizing:

Next step is implementation leading to institutionalizing wherein TPM becomes an organizational culture. Achieving PM award is the proof of reaching a satisfactory level.

STAGE B - Introduction Stage

This is a ceremony and we should invite all. Suppliers as they should know that we want quality supply from them. Related companies and affiliated companies who can be our customers, sisters concerns etc. Some may learn from us and some can help us and customers will get the communication from us that we care for quality output.

STAGE C - Implementation Stage

In this stage eight activities are carried which are called eight pillars in the development of TPM activity. Of these four activities are for establishing the system for production efficiency, one for initial control system of new products and equipment, one for improving the efficiency of administration and are for control of safety, sanitation as working environment.

STAGE D - Institutionalising Stage

By all these activities one would has reached maturity stage. Now is the time for applying for PM award. Also think of challenging level to which you can take this movement.

Chapter 5: TPM Pillars 1 to 4

PILLAR 1 - 5S

TPM starts with 5S. Problems cannot be clearly seen when the work place is unorganized. Cleaning and organizing the workplace helps the team to uncover problems. Making problems visible is the first step of improvement.

SEIRI - Sort out:

This means sorting and organizing the items as critical, important, frequently used items, useless, or items that are not needed as of now. Unwanted items can be salvaged. Critical items should be kept for use nearby and items that are not being used in near future, should be stored in some place. For this step, the worth of the item should be decided based on utility and not cost. As a result of this step, the search time is reduced.

SEITON - Organise:

The concept here is that "Each items has a place, and only one place". The items should be placed back after usage at the same place. To identify items easily, name plates and coloured tags has to be used. Vertical racks can be used for this purpose, and heavy items occupy the bottom position in the racks.

SEISO - Shine the workplace:

This involves cleaning the work place free of burrs, grease, oil, waste, scrap etc. No loosely hanging wires or oil leakage from machines.

SEIKETSU - Standardization:

Employees has to discuss together and decide on standards for keeping the work place, Machines and pathways neat and clean. This standards are implemented for whole organization and are tested/ Inspected randomly.

SHITSUKE - Self discipline:

Considering 5S as a way of life and bring about self-discipline among the employees of the organization. This includes wearing badges, following work procedures, punctuality, dedication to the organization etc.

PILLAR 2 - JISHU HOZEN (Autonomous maintenance)

This pillar is geared towards developing operators to be able to take care of small maintenance tasks, thus freeing up the skilled maintenance people to spend time on more value added activity and technical repairs. The operators are responsible for upkeep of their equipment to prevent it from deteriorating.

Policy:
   1.   Uninterrupted operation of equipments.

2. Flexible operators to operate and maintain other equipments.
3. Eliminating the defects at source through active employee participation.
4. Stepwise implementation of JH activities.

JISHU HOZEN Targets:

1. Prevent the occurrence of 1A / 1B because of JH.
2. Reduce oil consumption by 50%
3. Reduce process time by 50%
4. Increase use of JH by 50%

Steps in JISHU HOZEN:

1. Preparation of employees.
2. Initial cleanup of machines.
3. Take counter measures.
4. Fix tentative JH standards.
5. General inspection.
6. Autonomous inspection.
7. Standardization.
8. Autonomous management.

Each of the above mentioned steps is discussed in detail below.

Train the Employees

Educate the employees about TPM, Its advantages, JH advantages and Steps in JH. Educate the employees about abnormalities in equipments.

Initial cleanup of machines

Supervisor and technician should discuss and set a date for implementing step1

1. Arrange all items needed for cleaning.
2. On the arranged date, employees should clean the equipment completely with the help of maintenance department.
3. Dust, stains, oils and grease has to be removed.
4. The following are the things that has to be taken care while cleaning. They are:
   Oil leakage
   Loose wires
   Unfastened nuts and bolts
   Worn out parts.
5. After clean up problems are categorized and suitably tagged. White tags is place where problems can be solved by operators. Pink tag is placed where the aid of maintenance department is needed.
6. Contents of tag is transferred to a register.
7. Make note of area which were inaccessible.
8. Finally close the open parts of the machine and run the machine.

Counter Measures

1. Inaccessible regions had to be reached easily. E.g. If there are many screw to open a fly wheel door, hinge door can be used. Instead of opening a door for inspecting the machine, acrylic sheets can be used.

2. To prevent work out of machine parts necessary action must be taken.
3. Machine parts should be modified to prevent accumulation of dirt and dust.

Tentative Standard

1. JH schedule has to be made and followed strictly.
2. Schedule should be made regarding cleaning, inspection and lubrication and it also should include details like when, what and how.

General Inspection

1. The employees are trained in disciplines like Pneumatics, electrical, hydraulics, lubricant and coolant, drives, bolts, nuts and Safety.
2. This is necessary to improve the technical skills of employees and to use inspection manuals correctly.
3. After acquiring this new knowledge the employees should share this with others.
4. By acquiring this new technical knowledge, the operators are now well aware of machine parts.

Autonomous Inspection

1. New methods of cleaning and lubricating are used.
2. Each employee prepares his own autonomous chart/schedule in consultation with supervisor.

3. Parts which have never given any problem or part which don't need any inspection are removed from list permanently based on experience.
4. Including good quality machine parts. This avoid defects due to poor JH.
5. Inspection that is made in preventive maintenance is included in JH.
6. The frequency of cleanup and inspection is reduced based on experience.

Standardization

1. Up to the previous stem only the machinery / equipment was the concentration; however in this step the surroundings of machinery are organized. Necessary items should be organized, such that there is no searching and searching time is reduced.
2. Work environment is modified such that there is no difficulty in getting any item.
3. Everybody should follow the work instructions strictly.
4. Necessary spares for equipments is planned and procured.

Autonomous Management

1. OEE and OPE and other TPM targets must be achieved by continuous improve through Kaizen.
2. PDCA (Plan, Do, Check and Act) cycle must be implemented for Kaizen.

PILLAR 3 - KAIZEN

"Kai" means change, and "Zen" means good (for the better). Basically kaizen is for small improvements, but carried out on a continual basis and involve all people in the organization. Kaizen is opposite to big spectacular innovations. Kaizen requires no or little investment. The principle behind it is that "a very large number of small improvements are more effective in an organizational environment than a few improvements of large value. This pillar is aimed at reducing losses in the workplace that affect our efficiencies. By using a detailed and thorough procedure we eliminate losses in a systematic method using various Kaizen tools. These activities are not limited to production areas and can be implemented in administrative areas as well.

Kaizen Policy

1. Practice concepts of zero losses in every sphere of activity.
2. Relentless pursuit to achieve cost reduction targets in all resources.
3. Relentless pursuit to improve over all plant equipment effectiveness.
4. Extensive use of PM analysis as a tool for eliminating losses.
5. Focus of easy handling of operators.

Kaizen Target

Achieve and sustain zero loses with respect to minor stops, measurement and adjustments, defects and unavoidable downtimes. It also aims to achieve 30% manufacturing cost reduction.

Tools used in Kaizen

1. PM analysis.
2. Why - Why analysis.
3. Summary of losses.
4. Kaizen register.
5. Kaizen summary sheet.

The objective of TPM is maximization of equipment effectiveness. TPM aims at maximization of machine utilization and not merely machine availability maximization. As one of the pillars of TPM activities, Kaizen pursues efficient equipment, operator and material and energy utilization, that is extremes of productivity and aims at achieving substantial effects. Kaizen activities try to thoroughly eliminate 16 major losses.

16 Major losses in a organisation

Category 1: Losses that impede equipment efficiency.

1. Failure losses - Breakdown loss.
2. Setup / adjustment losses.
3. Cutting blade loss.
4. Start up loss.
5. Minor stoppage / Idling loss.
6. Speed loss - operating at low speeds.
7. Defect / rework loss.
8. Scheduled downtime loss.

Category 2: Loses that impede human work efficiency.

9. Management loss.
10. Operating motion loss.
11. Line organization loss.
12. Logistic loss.
13. Measurement and adjustment loss.

Category 3: Loses that impede effective use of production resources.

14. Energy loss.
15. Die, jig and tool breakage loss.
16. Yield loss.

PILLAR 4 - Planned Maintenance

It is aimed to have trouble free machines and equipments producing defect free products for total customer satisfaction. This breaks maintenance down into 4 "families" or groups which was defined in earlier chapter.

1. Preventive Maintenance
2. Breakdown Maintenance
3. Corrective Maintenance
4. Maintenance Prevention

With Planned Maintenance we evolve our efforts from a reactive to a proactive method and use trained maintenance staff to help train the operators to better maintain their equipment.

Policy:

1. Achieve and sustain availability of machines
2. Optimum maintenance cost.
3. Reduces spares inventory.
4. Improve reliability and maintainability of machines.

Target:

1. Zero equipment failure and break down.
2. Improve reliability and maintainability by 50%.
3. Reduce maintenance cost by 20%.
4. Ensure availability of spares all the time.

Six steps in Planned maintenance

1. Equipment evaluation and recoding present status.
2. Restore deterioration and improve weakness.
3. Building up information management system.
4. Prepare time based information system, select equipment, parts and members and map out plan.
5. Prepare predictive maintenance system by introducing equipment diagnostic techniques.
6. Evaluation of planned maintenance.

Chapter 6: TPM Pillars 5 to 8

PILLAR 5 - Quality Maintenance (QM)

It is aimed towards customer delight through highest quality through defect free manufacturing. Focus is on eliminating non-conformances in a systematic manner, much like Focused Improvement. We gain understanding of what parts of the equipment affect product quality and begin to eliminate current quality concerns, then move to potential quality concerns. Transition is from reactive to proactive (Quality Control to Quality Assurance).

QM activities is to set equipment conditions that preclude quality defects, based on the basic concept of maintaining perfect equipment to maintain perfect quality of products. The condition are checked and measure in time series to very that measure values are within standard values to prevent defects. The transition of measured values is watched to predict possibilities of defects occurring and to take counter measures before hand.

Policy:

1. Defect free conditions and control of equipments.
2. QM activities to support quality assurance.
3. Focus of prevention of defects at source.
4. Focus on poka-yoke. (fool proof system)
5. In-line detection and segregation of defects.

6. Effective implementation of operator quality assurance.

Target:

1. Achieve and sustain customer complaints at zero.
2. Reduce in-process defects by 50%.
3. Reduce cost of quality by 50%.

Data requirements:

Quality defects are classified as customer end defects and in house defects. For customer-end data, we have to get data on:
1. Customer end line rejection.
2. Field complaints.

In-house, data include data related to products and data related to process

Data related to product

1. Product wise defects.
2. Severity of the defect and its contribution - major/minor.
3. Location of the defect with reference to the layout.
4. Magnitude and frequency of its occurrence at each stage of measurement.
5. Occurrence trend in beginning and the end of each production/process/changes. (Like pattern change, ladle/furnace lining etc.)

6. Occurrence trend with respect to restoration of breakdown, modifications, periodical replacement of quality components.

Data related to processes

1. The operating condition for individual sub-process related to men, method, material and machine.
2. The standard settings/conditions of the sub-process.
3. The actual record of the settings/conditions during the defect occurrence.

PILLAR 6 - Training

It is aimed to have multi-skilled revitalized employees whose moral is high and who has eager to come to work and perform all required functions effectively and independently. Education is given to operators to upgrade their skill. It is not sufficient know only "Know-How" by they should also learn "Know-why". By experience they gain, "Know-How" to overcome a problem what to be done. This they do without knowing the root cause of the problem and why they are doing so. Hence it become necessary to train them on knowing "Know-why". The employees should be trained to achieve the four phases of skill. The goal is to create a factory full of experts. The different phase of skills are

Phase 1 : Do not know.
Phase 2 : Know the theory but cannot do.
Phase 3 : Can do but cannot teach

Phase 4 : Can do and also teach.

Policy

1. Focus on improvement of knowledge, skills and techniques.
2. Creating a training environment for self learning based on felt needs.
3. Training curriculum / tools /assessment etc conductive to employee revitalization.
4. Training to remove employee fatigue and make work enjoyable.

Target

1. Achieve and sustain downtime due to want men at zero on critical machines.
2. Achieve and sustain zero losses due to lack of knowledge / skills / techniques.
3. Aim for 100% participation in suggestion scheme.

Steps in Educating and training activities

1. Setting policies and priorities and checking present status of education and training.
2. Establishment of training system for operation and maintenance skill up gradation.
3. Training the employees for upgrading the operation and maintenance skills.
4. Preparation of training calendar.
5. Kick-off of the system for training.
6. Evaluation of activities and study of future approach.

PILLAR 7 - Office TPM

Office TPM should be started after activating four other pillars of TPM (JH, KK, QM, PM). Office TPM must be followed to improve productivity, efficiency in the administrative functions and identify and eliminate losses. This includes analyzing processes and procedures towards increased office automation. Office TPM addresses twelve major losses. They are

1. Processing loss.
2. Cost loss including in areas such as procurement, accounts, marketing, sales leading to high inventories.
3. Communication loss.
4. Idle loss.
5. Set-up loss.
6. Accuracy loss.
7. Office equipment breakdown.
8. Communication channel breakdown, telephone and fax lines.
9. Time spent on retrieval of information.
10. Non availability of correct on line stock status.
11. Customer complaints due to logistics.
12. Expenses on emergency dispatches and purchases.

How to start office TPM ?

A senior person from one of the support functions e.g. Head of Finance, MIS, Purchase etc should be heading the sub-committee. Members representing all support functions and people from Production and

Quality should be included in sub-committee. TPM co-ordinate plans and guides the sub-committee.

1. Providing awareness about office TPM to all support departments.
2. Helping them to identify P, Q, C, D, S, M in each function in relation to plant performance
3. Identify the scope for improvement in each function.
4. Collect relevant data.
5. Help them to solve problems in their circles.
6. Make up an activity board where progress is monitored on both sides - results and actions along with Kaizens.
7. Fan out to cover all employees and circles in all functions.

Kaizen topics for Office TPM

1. Inventory reduction.
2. Lead time reduction of critical processes.
3. Motion and space losses.
4. Retrieval time reduction.
5. Equalizing the work load.
6. Improving the office efficiency by eliminating the time loss on retrieval of information, by achieving zero breakdown of office equipment like telephone and fax lines.

Office TPM and its Benefits

1. Involvement of all people in support functions for focusing on better plant performance.

2. Better utilized work area.
3. Reduce repetitive work.
4. Reduced inventory levels in all parts of the supply chain.
5. Reduced administrative costs.
6. Reduced inventory carrying cost.
7. Reduction in number of files.
8. Reduction of overhead costs (to include cost of non-production/non capital equipment).
9. Productivity of people in support functions.
10. Reduction in breakdown of office equipment.
11. Reduction of customer complaints due to logistics.
12. Reduction in expenses due to emergency dispatches/purchases.
13. Reduced manpower.
14. Clean and pleasant work environment.

P Q C D S M in Office TPM

P - Production output lost due to want of material, Manpower productivity, Production output lost due to want of tools.

Q - Mistakes in preparation of cheques, bills, invoices, payroll, Customer returns/warranty attributable to BOPs, Rejection/rework in BOP's/job work, Office area rework.

C - Buying cost/unit produced, Cost of logistics - inbound/outbound, Cost of carrying inventory, Cost of communication, Demurrage costs.

D - Logistics losses (Delay in loading/unloading)

1. Delay in delivery due to any of the support functions.
2. Delay in payments to suppliers.
3. Delay in information.

S - Safety in material handling/stores/logistics, Safety of soft and hard data.

M - Number of kaizens in office areas.

How office TPM supports plant TPM

Office TPM supports the plant, initially in doing Jishu Hozen of the machines (after getting training of Jishu Hozen), as in Jishu Hozen at the:

1. Initial stages machines are more and manpower is less, so the help of commercial departments can be taken, for this.
2. Office TPM can eliminate the lodes on line for no material and logistics.

Extension of office TPM to suppliers and distributors

This is essential, but only after we have done as much as possible internally. With suppliers it will lead to on-time delivery, improved 'in-coming' quality and cost reduction. With distributors it will lead to accurate demand generation, improved secondary distribution and reduction in damages during storage and handling. In any case we will have to teach them based on our experience and practice and highlight gaps in the system which affect both sides. In case of some of the larger companies, they have started to support clusters of suppliers.

PILLAR 8 - Safety, Health and Environment

Target

1. Zero accident.
2. Zero health damage.
3. Zero fires.

In this area focus is on to create a safe workplace and a surrounding area that is not damaged by our process or procedures. This pillar will play an active role in each of the other pillars on a regular basis.

A committee is constituted for this pillar which comprises representative of officers as well as workers. The committee is headed by Senior vice President Technical or Technical Director. Utmost importance to Safety is given in the plant. Manager (Safety) is looking after functions related to safety. To create awareness among employees various competitions like safety slogans, Quiz, Drama, Posters, etc. related to safety can be organized at regular intervals.

Today, with competition in industry at an all time high, TPM may be the only thing that stands between success and total failure for some companies. It has been proven to be a program that works. It can be adapted to work not only in industrial plants, but in construction, building maintenance, transportation, and in a variety of other situations. Employees must be educated and convinced that TPM is not just another "program of the month" and that management is totally committed to the program and the extended time frame necessary for full implementation. If everyone involved in a TPM program does his or her part, an unusually high rate of return compared to resources invested may be expected.

Chapter 7: Environmental Impacts of TPM

As we stated in earlier chapters Total Productive Maintenance (TPM) seeks to engage all levels and functions in an organization to maximize the overall effectiveness of production equipment. This method further tunes up existing processes and equipment by reducing mistakes and accidents. Whereas maintenance departments are the traditional centre of preventive maintenance programs, TPM seeks to involve workers in all departments and levels, from the plant-floor to senior executives, to ensure effective equipment operation.

Autonomous maintenance, a key aspect of TPM, trains and focuses workers to take care of the equipment and machines with which they work. TPM addresses the entire production system lifecycle and builds a solid, plant-floor based system to prevent accidents, defects, and breakdowns. TPM focuses on preventing breakdowns (preventive maintenance), "mistake-proofing" equipment (or poka-yoke) to eliminate product defects or to make maintenance easier (corrective maintenance), designing and installing equipment that needs little or no maintenance (maintenance prevention), and quickly repairing equipment after breakdowns occur (breakdown maintenance).

The goal is the total elimination of all losses, including breakdowns, equipment setup and adjustment losses, idling and minor stoppages, reduced speed, defects and rework, spills and process upset conditions, and startup and yield losses. The ultimate goals of TPM are zero equipment breakdowns and zero product defects, which lead to improved utilization of production assets and plant capacity.

Implications for Environmental Performance

Potential Benefits

Properly maintaining equipment and systems helps reduce defects that result from a process. A reduction in defects can, in turn, help eliminate waste from processes in three fundamental ways:

1. Fewer defects decreases the number of products that must be scrapped.
2. Fewer defects also means that the raw materials, energy, and resulting waste associated with the scrap are eliminated.
3. Fewer defects decreases the amount of energy, raw material, and wastes that are used or generated to fix defective products that can be re-worked.

TPM can increase the longevity of equipment, thereby decreasing the need to purchase and/or make replacement equipment. This, in turn, reduces the environmental impacts associated with raw materials and manufacturing processes needed to produce new equipment.

TPM often attempts to decrease the number and severity of equipment spills, leaks, and upset conditions. This typically reduces the solid and hazardous wastes (e.g., contaminated rags and adsorbent pads) resulting from spills and leaks and their clean-up.

Potential Shortcomings

Failure to consider the environmental aspects or impacts associated with equipment during mistake-proofing and equipment efficiency improvement can leave potential waste minimization and pollution prevention opportunities on the table. For example, equipment can often be modified to reduce or eliminate spills, leaks, overspray, and misting that increase clean-up needs.

TPM can result in increased use of cleaning supplies, particularly if the route-cause of unclean conditions are not addressed. Cleaning supplies may contain solvents and/or chemicals that can result in air emissions or increased waste generation.

Method and Implementation Approach

TPM is focused primarily on keeping machinery functioning optimally and minimizing equipment breakdowns and associated waste by making equipment more efficient, conducting preventative, corrective, and autonomous maintenance, mistake-proofing equipment, and effectively managing safety and environmental issues. TPM seeks to eliminate six major losses that can result from faulty equipment or operation, as summarized below.

Six major losses that can result from poor maintenance, faulty equipment or inefficient operation.

Type of Loss	Costs to Organization
Unexpected breakdown losses	Results in equipment downtime for repairs. Costs can include downtime (and lost production opportunity or yields), labour, and spare parts.
Set-up and adjustment losses	Results in lost production opportunity (yields) that occurs during product changeovers, shift change or other changes in operating conditions.
Stoppage losses	Results in frequent production downtime from zero to 10 minutes in length and that are difficult to record manually. As a result, these losses are usually hidden from efficiency reports and are built into machine capabilities but can cause substantial equipment downtime and lost production opportunity.
Speed losses	Results in productivity losses when equipment must be slowed down to prevent quality defects or minor stoppages. In most cases, this loss is not recorded because the equipment continues to operate.
Quality defect losses	Results in off-spec production and defects due to equipment malfunction or poor performance, leading to output which must be reworked or scrapped as waste.
Equipment and capital investment losses	Results in wear and tear on equipment that reduces its durability and productive life span, leading to more frequent capital investment in replacement equipment.

Organizations typically pursue the four techniques below to implement TPM. Kaizen events can be used to focus organizational attention on implementing these techniques.

1. Efficient Equipment

The best way to increase equipment efficiency is to identify the losses, among the six described above, that are hindering performance. To measure overall equipment effectiveness, a TPM index, Overall Equipment Effectiveness (OEE) is used. OEE is calculated by multiplying (each as a percentage), overall equipment availability, performance and product quality rate. With these figures, the amount of time spent on each of the six big losses, and where most attention needs to be focused, can be determined. It is estimated that most companies can realize a 15-25 percent increase in equipment efficiency rates within three years of adopting TPM.

2. Effective Maintenance

Thorough and routine maintenance is a critical aspect of TPM. First and foremost, TPM trains equipment operators to play a key role in preventive maintenance by carrying out "autonomous maintenance" on a daily basis. Typical daily activities include precision checks, lubrication, parts replacement, simple repairs, and abnormality detection. Workers are also encouraged to conduct corrective maintenance, designed to further keep equipment from breaking down, and to facilitate inspection, repair and use. Corrective maintenance includes recording the results of daily inspections, and regularly considering and submitting maintenance improvement ideas.

3. Mistake-Proofing

Known as poka-yoke in lean manufacturing contexts; mistake-proofing is the application of simple "fail-safing" mechanisms designed to make mistakes impossible or at least easy to detect and correct. Poka-yoke devices fall into two major categories; prevention and detection.

    a. A prevention device is one that makes it impossible for a machine or machine operator to make a mistake. For example, many automobiles have "shift locks" that prevent a driver from shifting into reverse unless their foot is on the brake.

    b. A detection device signals the user when a mistake has been made, so that the user can quickly correct the problem. In automobiles, a detection device might be a warning buzzer indicating that keys have been inadvertently left in the ignition.

4. Safety Management

The fundamental principle behind TPM safety and environmental management activities is addressing potentially dangerous conditions and activities before they cause accidents, damage, and unanticipated costs. Like maintenance, safety activities under TPM are to be carried out continuously and systematically. Focus areas includes.

a. The development of safety checklists (e.g., to detect leaks, unusual equipment vibration, or static electricity).
b. The standardization of operations (e.g., materials handling and transport, use of protective clothing, etc.)
c. Coordinating non-repetitive maintenance tasks (e.g., especially those involving electrical hazards, toxic substances, open flames, etc.).
d. In many cases, equipment can be modified to minimize the likelihood of equipment malfunction and upset conditions.

Chapter 8: TPM and OEE

Total Productive Maintenance (TPM) challenges the view that maintenance is no more than a function that operates in the background and only appears when needed. The objective of TPM is to engender a sense of joint responsibility between supervision, operators and maintenance workers, not simply to keep machines running smoothly, but also to extend and optimise their performance overall. The results are proving to be remarkable.

The goals of TPM are measured using an Overall Equipment Effectiveness (OEE) ratio.

OEE = availability x performance x Quality rate.

Availability = Available time – downtime x 100

Available time

Downtime can be calculated by adding together the amounts of time lost due to equipment failures, set-up and adjustment, and idling and minor stoppages.

Performance rate = Ideal cycle time x Processed Quantity x 100

Operating time

Speed losses are calculated by combining time lost due to idling and minor stoppages and time lost due to reductions in speed.

Quality rate = Processed Quantity − defective quantity x 100

Processed quantity

Defective quantity is calculated by combining defects in process start-up and reduced yield.

Typical calculations for OEE prior to the implementation of Just in Time related strategies usually range between 40% and 50% with the former being the more normal. Experience indicates that it is possible to raise this to between 80% and 90% in a period of some two to three years from start up; however, the improvement will usually follow an almost exponential upward curve with the bulk of the gains being in the latter part of the period.

Do Not Be Misled by O.E.E

Overall equipment effectiveness (O.E.E.) has been used as one of the more important "maintenance metrics" since Total Productive Maintenance (TPM) came to the U.S. in the late 1980s. O.E.E. is the primary measure used in TPM to identify and quantify the major equipment-related losses and a metric for rating "equipment effectiveness." O.E.E. has become widely used in many plants with or without the elements of TPM in place since the early years of TPM to quantify equipment effectiveness losses. This usage has also caused some confusion and has led to many misuses of the O.E.E. percentage calculation.

The early Toyota Production System focused on "eliminating waste to reduce cost." O.E.E. was initially developed to identify the "major losses" in equipment performance and reliability. TPM then became a "company-wide approach to eliminating the major equipment losses." O.E.E. addressed whether the equipment was doing the right things.

O.E.E. grew out of the "Japanese Quality Revolution" in the 1950s, 1960s, and beyond. The Deming cycle (plan - do - check - act), based on the "scientific method," required the collection of data to define and characterize the nature of the problem to be solved.

Let the Confusion Begin

This is where all the confusion begins. O.E.E. percentages became a metric to compare current equipment performance to world-class performance. The measure of 85% equipment effectiveness became known as "world-class O.E.E." Once used as a benchmarking score for "world-class", O.E.E. became used as a way to compare one piece of equipment to another, even though the equipment performed different functions in a different process, or even in a different plant. Once this basic calculation became more widespread, O.E.E. started being used to specify "Overall Plant Effectiveness" (O.P.E.) by using an aggregate score for all equipment in the plant. O.E.E. and then O.P.E. have become widely used to compare current levels of maintenance effectiveness and equipment performance to "world-class" levels, and even a "club" to punish those whose

O.E.E. slips. All of these uses are inaccurate, unfair comparisons, and they are a gross misuse of the original purposes of O.E.E.

O.E.E. Data

O.E.E. was designed and developed to characterize and communicate the major equipment-related losses; by capturing equipment performance and reliability data and classifying it as a specific "availability, efficiency, or quality loss," Pareto charts could be developed to communicate the "major losses" for focused improvement. This O.E.E. data could then measure and communicate the effectiveness of the focused improvement efforts, the countermeasures put in place to eliminate the major loss, or problem, and to tap the "hidden capacity."

O.E.E. Percentage Rating

The O.E.E. percentage calculation (O.E.E. rating) served no purpose other than a very high-level indicator of performance improvement or degradation. Today, entirely too much emphasis is placed on trending and analyzing the "calculated O.E.E. rating." The original intent is lost in many cases.

O.E.E. is a process for characterizing and communicating the major equipment-related losses. If it is only used as a "calculated rating," it cannot be used by reliability professionals, operators or mechanics to quickly determine and eliminate the root causes of poor performance - as it should be used.

O.E.E. as a calculated rating is not entirely accurate. The basic factors of "availability, efficiency, and quality losses" assume that each of these losses is equally important. This is not universally true. It is a rare situation in manufacturing that a 1% downtime loss has the same business or financial impact as a 1% efficiency loss or a 1% quality loss. The O.E.E. calculation assumes equal weight of each factor - a dangerous assumption in return-on-investment calculations.

O.E.E. should not be used to compare machine-to-machine or process-to-process unless they are identical. O.E.E. should not be used to compare plant to plant or to specify "world-class" performance and reliability. There is no credible "world-class" O.E.E. percentage threshold - only a misconception.

O.E.E. is Not a Maintenance Measure

O.E.E. is not a measure of "maintenance effectiveness." It is a measure of the factors that determine "equipment effectiveness." For example, of the major losses listed in earlier chapter of this book, "maintenance" is typically in direct control of only two: planned maintenance, breakdowns and failures. Quite often, these two major losses are also impacted by the operations roles. Maintenance alone cannot address all of the major losses captured for O.E.E. This is why O.E.E. is used in Total Productive Maintenance where the entire organization focuses on eliminating the major losses.

O.E.E. data collection, analysis, reporting, and trending provide the fundamental underlying basis for improving equipment effectiveness by eliminating the major equipment-related losses. O.E.E. data very quickly leads to root-cause identification and elimination. O.E.E. data then answers the question, "Did we eliminate the root cause of poor equipment performance?" O.E.E. data is the means to an end; improving overall equipment effectiveness.

Calculating O.E.E. removes our efforts further from eliminating the major losses to comparing O.E.E. scores and the related punishment and praises as O.E.E. falls or improves. O.E.E. scores are neither a means to an end or an end. Be careful. It is a measure of "equipment effectiveness," not a measure maintenance effectiveness. Don't be misled by O.E.E.

Chapter 9: Operators as a Maintenance Resource

This chapter is a case study and interview response from one of the maintenance practitioners at the headquarter of a very large multi-national oil and gas group.

This facility was the technical headquarters of a very large multi-national oil and gas group of companies. From these offices, the corporate staff provided technical support to a large number of exploration and production facilities, refineries, gas plants, and chemical plants located around the world. A small maintenance and reliability team provided a benchmarking and consultancy service to the refineries and gas plants. The team identified maintenance best practices for sharing within the group to promote increased profitability and plant availability.

I was one of a team of experienced maintenance practitioners in the corporate headquarters, who provided technical support to the refineries. (said the practitioner interviewed.)

We focused on improving reliability and maintenance performance. We developed a maintenance and reliability performance appraisal program with which we could identify improvement actions. The client refinery agreed to execute the recommended actions within a time frame and with a clear implementation plan.

The program was carried out during a visit to the client refinery, jointly with selected members of the client's own staff. This collaborative effort tapped their knowledge and experience while giving them a sense of ownership of the project.

Execution of Maintenance Work

We selected efficiency of execution of maintenance work as one of the target areas for performance improvement. The key success factors for this are:

1. Good planning, scheduling, and resource optimization.
2. Full and effective utilization of resources.

Operator Workload

When we looked for underutilized resources, plant operators stood out like sore thumbs. An internationally respected firm specializing in refinery performance benchmarking confirmed this view. In their studies, they found that at least 25% of plant operators' time is unstructured and, therefore, can be utilized productively for carrying out certain types of maintenance work.

Refinery managements are generally reluctant to accept this observation.

The subject of operator numbers is traditionally closely protected, influenced by a perceived concern for operational safety.

He said during one of my visits to a client refinery, this topic came up for discussion in the course of the performance review. There were four participants from the client's side: the operations manager, the maintenance and engineering manager, the projects manager, and the chief inspector. I could not convince them of the validity of the observation. Not unexpectedly, the operations manager held the strongest objections.

I challenged him to call the front line operations supervisor to the forum and carry out a tally of operators' defined duties and time spent on these duties.

He accepted the challenge. To the best of our knowledge, this was the first time that such an exercise was carried out in this manner. None of us foresaw, or could have foretold the results.

The Challenge

The operations manager invited the shift supervisor for this exercise. When he learned what he had to do, the shift supervisor requested that his senior panel operator also be allowed to come and help him. We scheduled the exercise to take place after the shift change when both people would be free from their duties.

The two men came at the appointed time. Both were a bit nervous to face the forum in which their big boss, the operations manager, was also present.

On my suggestion, the operations manager himself took the lead in developing the tally.

The participants themselves found the result of the exercise incredible. Indeed, they could account for less than 75% of the time as shown in the tally, and this included some maintenance work already being done by operators.

This convinced them to accept additional alternative work for operators.

Type of Maintenance Work for Operators

Operators' unstructured time should be utilized only for alternative work, which we will call front line maintenance.

1. Derive the tasks from RCM/RBI analysis results. These will be preventive maintenance tasks identified by a review in which operators have themselves participated; hence they are more likely to accepted. Leave the specialist tasks for specialists.
2. The order of preference is preventive maintenance, then condition monitoring, and last of all corrective maintenance.
3. The primary task of the operator is to operate the plant safely. Therefore, only interruptible maintenance tasks are suitable as front-line

work. This policy will enable release of operators should operators be required urgently to handle any emerging operational situation.

4. The available operator time is treated as a maintenance resource. It is planned, scheduled, and accounted for, as for the regular maintainers.

Before operators can start doing some of these tasks, we gave them some focused training.

Result

The refinery now uses nearly 25% of their operator time in front-line maintenance activities.

Lessons

1. Use of resources can be critically scrutinized to reveal under-utilization.
2. To be useful, this should be done with an open mind with the full participation of the relevant parties.
3. Operators can carry out useful maintenance work after minimal training, without jeopardizing their primary duty of operating the plant safely.

Principles

We will always find many defenders of the status-quo. Challenging these and understanding the factual situation can help demolish such citadels.

Chapter 10: Things Your Equipment Operators Can Do to Improve Reliability

There is no denying that the equipment that makes your products and the operators who operate it are the most valuable assets an organization has. So unless you are actually manufacturing product and shipping it, you are overhead. From the janitorial services to the CEO, you are just another additional cost that has to be included in the cost of the product.

So why, then, do our most valuable assets receive so little training, are swapped around like poker chips in Vegas, and are often expected to do little more than push a button and babysit the machine? Given this prevalent management philosophy, we then struggle to understand why our continuous improvement efforts fail to take hold and come to the conclusion that the equipment we purchased is junk and/or our people don't know how to operate it.

Well folks, it's time to wake up. Here are 10 things your operators can do today to improve the reliability of your equipment.

1. Keep it Clean

There is a mountain of data that supports the fact that clean machines run significantly better. We need to give our manufacturing equipment operators time to clean their equipment and perform routine operator care tasks during each shift. These tasks need to be clearly identified with qualitative descriptions that give specifics regarding what type of cleaning agent, what type of cloth and what the area should look like when the task is complete. If this sounds a bit excessive, try this on one of your critical assets. In three months, you will definitely see a return on investment in increased productivity and reduced maintenance costs.

2. Insist on Training

Trained equipment operators understand how their equipment works, know the performance standards they need to maintain so equipment operates properly, and know how to troubleshoot and address any problem they might encounter with their machine. Those without training fumble through the day; they know where three buttons are on the operator screen; stop, start and reset. They shut their machine down and contact maintenance for simple problems, and they struggle with product changes. If you are an equipment operator, you have to insist on formal training. Watching someone else run a machine for a couple of hours or days IS NOT formal training. Chances are, that person was never formally trained either. Insist for your own safety, because you love your parents, spouse, children, or friends. Operators who are not formally trained are much more likely to suffer a severe injury or fatality on the job.

3. Stop the Musical Chairs

The theory that we need to train all our operators to run every piece of equipment continues to cycle through the manufacturing community every few years. To any manager who believes in this foolish concept, here is a challenge. Put on some work clothes, take a month out of your busy schedule and try this out yourself. See what you can learn in a few days on each machine and decide for yourself if you feel confident in what you are being paid to do; having your operators change machines on a regular basis makes about as much sense as it would to have NASCAR drivers drive someone else's car in the race each Sunday. It doesn't work well and, once again, it's not safe! As proof, operators should begin taking data regarding how effectively the machines run when we change operators. In the same way that automated equipment doesn't like to stop and start, operators are less effective in their work when they are required to change to a new machine. It's understandable to have a few people who can operate more than one or two machines, but these people are called team or line leaders.

4. Learn Statistical Process Control (SPC)

The next step beyond learning how to operate your machine is learning when to make adjustments based on operating and product parameters. SPC is a very powerful tool used mostly by the folks who work in product quality, but it can be just as powerful, if not more so, when put into the hands of operators who are looking at learning more about the machine or process they operate.

5. Get Serious About Root Cause Analysis (RCA)

RCA has been getting a bad name lately, with experienced operators using a simple 5 Why process and doing two or three RCAs a week, but nothing ever comes of them. In most cases, RCA is ineffective because the triggers are set way too low or people rush through the process and look for a single solution. Your lead operators or team leaders should be leading your RCAs and if you didn't find the correct solution, it's because you didn't identify all of the causes.

6. Bring Precision into Product Change

More than half of organizations report struggling with product changes. Even stranger than this, the companies that do the most product changes tend to struggle the most. One would think if performing product changes was a daily part of your work schedule, you would naturally become good at them; however, the reality is that while we expect our machines to perform precision work, we rarely apply precision techniques to our machines when it comes time to perform a product change. Managers have somehow come to believe that using a permanent marker to make a black mark that is nearly one-fourth inches in width on a piece of sheet metal will result in a tremendously accurate product change. Make six other marks in different colours, don't label any of them and do this in six or eight different stations, then sit back in your office and wonder why your operators struggle at each product change. Operators should be vocal about bringing precision techniques into each product change; the use of jigs and blanks will go a long way in reducing the cycle time for product change and improve the precision to a point of one and done.

7. Get Involved in the Reliability Tools RCM and TPM

If you are really interested in how your machine was designed and how it was intended to be operated and maintained, volunteer to become part of a reliability centered maintenance (RCM) or total productive maintenance (TPM) team. Both of these tools take operators to the next level. For example, operators who have participated in RCM analyses for critical machines report having a better understanding about how the equipment was designed to work and why it was critical to inspect and record things like pressures, temperatures and flows on each machine.

8. Drive Decisions with Data

For some reason, those who work in the operations and maintenance departments believe if they complain long enough and loud enough about the problems their machines are having, then someone in management will finally do something about it. The reality is this thinking could not be further from the truth. If you want to see changes, you need to bring data to the table. In your job, you are surrounded by useful data. Each day you record useful data, but chances are that very little is done with that data. Learn the art of business by driving change through data supported decisions.

9. Make Safety First

While some believe reliability and safety go hand in hand, the reality is reliability depends on safety. If your equipment is not safe, then it cannot be reliable. On the other hand, at plants where reliability is a big issue, the pressure is on operators to keep equipment up and running. This can result in operators cutting corners with safety to maintain throughput. It is important for everyone to understand that in order to have safe and reliable equipment, everyone has to do the right things when it comes to safety. Cutting corners on safety to keep equipment running doesn't help anyone and puts personal health and safety at risk. If you have been cutting corners on safety at your plant, do the right thing starting today; shut it off and demand that someone make it right.

10. Follow the Checklist

If your job is to operate a piece of equipment; it doesn't matter if it is a Boeing 747, a chemical reactor, paper machine, steam turbine, or flour mill; you should be using a detailed checklist to start up the machine, shut it down, make sure it is fit for use, or perform a product change. The checklist wasn't created because someone thinks they are smarter than you or that equipment operators are dummies; the checklist was created to ensure we do our jobs in the correct order and sequence to guarantee safety and reliability. If you are still sceptical, think for a moment about how much training the average commercial airline pilot has to go through to become certified to pilot or co-pilot an aircraft. Does anyone doubt their intelligence? Yet each and every flight, the pilots go through a detailed checklist to ensure the aircraft they are operating is fit for use.

The best equipment operators enjoy their work, see the value in what they do and, quite often, have some great ideas on how to improve both processes and equipment and they do this while working rotating shifts, often scheduled to work while their children and families get on school buses, or play in ballgames and concerts. Yet, when something goes wrong in the middle of the night, while engineers and managers are home sleeping, they are the first people we seek to blame for the upset.

These top 10 items for equipment operators will improve the lives of everyone who work at a manufacturing facility and for those who question the important work of operators and maintenance people, then perhaps they should try working at least three months of back-to-back rotating shifts to truly appreciate the sacrifices these people make to keep things running.

Chapter 11: One Point Lesson

What is a One Point Lesson (OPL)?

A One Point Lesson is a 5 to 10 minutes learning tool, which normally take less than 15 minutes to write. It is a lesson on a single topic/point, on one sheet of paper. It normally consists of 80% diagram and 20% words all produced by hand. It is generally prepared by supervisors or group leaders and sometimes by operators.

When to use it?

Whenever an important message must be communicated and understood.

What does it achieve?

An OPL quickly enables a team to share key learning and builds on a common understanding of the systems and standards that apply to a work area. When properly managed, they support greater transparency of knowledge and help to rapidly bring new people in an area up to speed.

1. To pass on better knowledge.
2. Strengthen the understanding for functions of machines and lines.
3. Improve knowledge about maintenance defect prevention.

Types of OPL

1. **Basic information sheet:** Essential basic information; practical know-how and know-how of methods:
   a. Maintenance activities as e.g. filter changing.
   b. Small repair works.
   c. Setting of machine functions.
   d. Cleaning and checking.
   e. Lubricating.
   f. Reason for quality loss.

2. Problem case study sheet: Teaches how to prevent recurrence of an actual equipment problem.

3. Improvement / Kaizen lessons study case: Describes the approach and key measures in a successful improvement case study.

Key points to remember when writing OPL's

1. Only One Point illustrated on a single sheet of paper.
2. As many senses as possible should be addressed.
3. It must be written As Simple As Possible.
4. It should take approximately 15 minutes to write using a pencil, pen or felt tips.
5. When words are used, they should be ALL capitals.

When considering the condition or performance of an asset we often forget the contribution that our workforce can make. The people who are closest to the human interface with the physical asset often have a wealth of knowledge and information regarding how the asset is performing. But how can we tap into this free and often vital information? One such approach is a "TPM 1-Point Lesson". It requires just two enablers to be in place. You need a motivated and empowered workforce. How important is this to achieving a successful asset Management Company?

It should be noted that although human factors such as leadership, motivation and culture are largely outside the scope of this Publicly Available Specification, they are critical to the successful achievement of asset management and require due consideration. This is applicable to the organisations' managers, employees, contractors and suppliers.

A key characteristic of successful asset management is consistently making sound decisions and good compromises, and carrying out the appropriate tasks at the right time and at the optimum level of expenditure. Above all it requires the commitment of top management, and it is unlikely that an organisation will successfully integrate and optimise their asset management without such commitment. It also requires a motivated workforce supported by an effective asset management system, adequate and appropriate information and only thereafter, the usage of various asset management tools.

For some organisations this may require a change in culture and it might challenge existing ways of thinking and working.

The benefits of using Total Productive Maintenance techniques is well understood and is often seen as one of the tools capable of delivering an empowered and motivated workforce. These simple but effective techniques get the involvement of those very important people, who operate the key human interface with the asset. A TPM 1-point lesson is just one of the many tools that can be used to improve knowledge and understanding of the condition and performance of an asset on a day-to-day basis. The approach engages the front-line operations and technicians and encourages them to get involved in the continuous improvement of the asset. By simply passing on good ideas, maintenance interventions can be optimised to ensure their maximum impact on either the performance or condition of the assets.

Chapter 12: Difficulties in Implementing TPM

It is important to understand up front that Total Productive Maintenance is the most difficult of all the "lean tools" to implement in companies for two reasons:

1. A TPM implementation requires the greatest amount of culture change (as compared to implementing other lean tools) from different groups of people within the organization almost simultaneously.

2. Of all of the areas of potential lean process improvement within the four walls of an organization, the maintenance of our equipment is the area which is the furthest behind.

Fortunately, the payback from this implementation in terms of on-time delivery, reduced scrap, improved productivity and improved associate moral; is probably greater than any of the other lean tools.

Let's review both of these challenging implementation issues and consider possible solutions.

As we look at the organizational culture required for the TPM implementation, it is important to remember and review the four components of a successful lean transformation.

To successfully implement TPM (as well as any of the other lean tools), it must be built on a foundation of a lean culture and supported by the lean policy deployment part of lean planning.

The development of a lean culture starts with the establishment of behavioural expectations. Such expectations, or codes of conduct, set the culture baseline. An excellent example is shown below:

For TPM to be successful, two additional cultural changes must occur:

First: Management, in most organizations, has always considered the maintenance department to be a "necessary evil", an undesirable "indirect" expense. Management has failed to properly lead and manage the maintenance activity. As a result of this treatment, maintenance:

1. Wants to be located as far away from production and management as possible.
2. Has little regard for the production process.
3. Considers themselves "on call".
4. Uses a "fire-fighting/chicken-wire repair" maintenance strategy.
5. Makes excuses for a lack of maintenance improvements.

This must change. In lean, maintenance activities are known to be the foundation of creating world-class manufacturing processes.

Second: Is the development of respect for our manufacturing equipment and the products they produce. Often, U.S. and UK organizations buy new equipment, ignore or are unconcerned about proper maintenance procedures and schedules and then proceed to run the equipment into the ground. Then everyone stands around complaining that what the organization needs is new equipment. They buy new equipment and the cycle repeats.

While visiting Japan, we were told by a Japanese plant manager, who was watching a brand new piece of equipment being unloaded at his facility, that "this was the worst condition this piece of equipment would ever be in." This reflected a cultural respect for how important the equipment was to their success and how the Japanese never let equipment deteriorate but always try to improve it or make it better (easier to operate, easier to maintain, etc.).

Additionally, top management must:

1. Make TPM a part of their policy deployment goals.
2. Support the creation of a full-time certified lean facilitator position (organizations with more than 100 people).
3. Support, encourage and discuss the organizational role and culture changes that will be required during this transition.
4. Ignore the red flags that TPM will create if the organization is using a "standard cost" accounting system.
5. Recognize a world-class-level TPM implementation can take many years (again, of

all the lean tools/activities, maintenance is the furthest behind).

Other TPM Implementation Considerations

1. Some thoughts on supporting the maintenance department culture change:

   a. Treat/respect maintenance as the foundation of our processes (not as an indirect cost!).
   b. Move maintenance to the centre of the processes (if required, 5-S during the move).
   c. Assign maintenance directly to cells, production lines and value streams (indirectly to maintenance manager).

2. Five potential maintenance strategies

Breakdown: Wait until it breaks then scramble or use the "fire-fighting" strategy, also known as reactive maintenance (this is what many organization are currently doing).

Preventive (planned downtime): Periodic or scheduled maintenance; e.g., oiling, greasing, filter changes, etc., to prevent premature wear and breakdowns, combined with periodic major inspections and overhauls, which prevent equipment performance deterioration.

Predictive: Repair or replace components before failure based on historical information, monitoring equipment operation or life cycles. Life cycles can be based on:

a. Number of cycles.
b. Operating time in minutes or hours.
c. Calendar time.
d. Component wear data.
e. Variations in component operating parameters.

Corrective or improvement: Use of "root cause" analysis to determine why a component wore out or failed, followed by equipment modifications or upgrades to prevent recurrence.

Maintenance Prevention: Design or specification of equipment components that do not require maintenance. This can include the design or specification of equipment that is easy to clean, inspect and lubricate. Preventive and predictive strategies can account for 75 to 90 percent of all improvement in the short term.

3. The key to an effective preventive maintenance component within the TPM initiative is the machine operators. Up to 75 percent of breakdowns can be detected and prevented by well-trained associates.

4. Component failure analysis studies indicate that from 60 to 75 percent of all equipment mechanical failures are a result of lubrication failure (contaminated, wrong type, inadequate or excessive).

5. The cost of a TPM program is optimized (between spending too much and not spending enough) when roughly 90 percent of all maintenance activities are planned and 10 percent are unplanned.

6. Often, a good place to start your TPM overall equipment effectiveness (OEE) measurement system is with equipment availability.

7. Purchase a TPM computer program only after a manual system, which meets the organization data management and analysis requirements, has been developed.

8. Equipment builders who do not support TPM efforts on their already purchased equipment should not be considered for future equipment purchases.

9. Consider using a measurement system like the one used to measure lean supplier performance:

Chapter 13: Toyota and TPM

Working with little inventory and stopping production when there is a problem causes instability and a sense of urgency among workers. In mass production, when a machine goes down, there is no sense of urgency; excess inventory will keep the operation running while maintenance fixes the problem. In lean production, when an operator shuts down production to fix a problem, the line will soon stop producing, creating a crisis and a sense of urgency. A properly implemented and maintained Total Productive Maintenance System (TPM) will provide the needed stability for lean production.

A little more than 30 years ago, an automotive supplier company in Japan (Nippon Denso) realized that until you address and systematically eliminate the causes of poor equipment performance, you cannot deliver to your customers "just in time," improve quality levels, lower operating costs or improve profits. In 1969, the ideas of Total Productive Maintenance, facilitated by Seiichi Nakajima, helped take the Toyota Production System to the next level. Since the Toyota Production System was focused on the absolute elimination of waste to reduce manufacturing cost, TPM was designed to systematically identify and eliminate equipment losses (downtime, inefficiency, defects). In implementing lean manufacturing practices, machine availability plays an important role. Preventive maintenance is a key aspect in ensuring machine availability. This practice achieves maximum efficient usage of machines through total employee involvement.

Toyota has created an organizational culture that encourages employee participation, which is essential for successful TPM. Group activities are promoted among the shop-floor team members. The knowledge base of all the employees is used to improve equipment reliability and productivity thereby lowering maintenance and operating costs. Two other important aspects of TPM are training and open communication between operators and engineering. Production personnel are trained to perform routine maintenance.

The traditional approach to preventive maintenance is a clear-cut division of labour.

1. Machine operators perform routine maintenance functions.
2. Maintenance technicians are responsible for specialized maintenance and for improving maintainability.
3. Engineering is responsible for improving the process.

This practice is not capable of achieving the TPM targets, as there is a lack of communication between operating and maintenance teams.

Nippon Denso came out with an alternative approach of appointing a machine technician (MT) that supports communication between operators and maintenance. The responsibilities of the MT were to perform minor maintenance and repair tasks. These MTs underwent classroom training on tool finishing and fitting as well as on-the-job training. On-the-job training gave them exposure to machines and helped them gain expertise in their area.

There are two different types of philosophies of TPM. Firstly, there is the centralized maintenance approach. This requires maintenance personnel to be cross-trained, thus providing flexibility of using a number of workers for scheduling maintenance tasks. This flexibility is essential because as workers move up in seniority level, there is a tendency to opt for convenient shifts instead of third shift.

The second approach is decentralization. As personnel become more experienced in one functional area, they gain more expertise. Sometimes it requires six months of training before a person becomes proficient in a new area. Thus, frequent job rotations may result in under-utilization of skills gained through training. A good example of this type of approach is at Honda Motors for its three departments; suspension assembly, facilities and engine assembly. Each department has a separate maintenance team. The reasons for this shift were the need for 12 to 18 months of training in each area, and local regulations required maintenance to take place only on weekends and shutdowns.

Toyota has a centralized maintenance function with cross-trained employees. The benefits of decentralized maintenance are derived from the use of MTs. These MT's are experts in their areas;

however, availability of limited maintenance personnel necessitates cross-trained employees.

Toyota also collects data for analysis and trend establishment. Sufficient data on the trend and pattern of equipment's performance should be available for identifying and setting up standards and procedures for preventive maintenance. This data would also be useful in determining costs of preventive maintenance and repairs, run-to-failure vs. preventive maintenance, and failure history.

Organizations also need to evaluate the impact of organizational structure and processes on preventive maintenance. Change in these can have an overwhelming impact on employee moral, efficiency and effectiveness. As Toyota has shown, preventive maintenance management calls for long-term commitment to the goal and pays dividends in the long run.

Chapter 14: How to Implement TPM

As we conduct lean assessments at manufacturing facilities throughout the UK, I have noticed organizations increasingly embracing lean concepts; but one key area that often falls by the wayside is equipment maintenance. I repeatedly see facilities in which there is a complacent attitude about equipment maintenance and reliability. "Equipment is expected to fail." Maintenance is primarily reactive. Where they exist, preventive maintenance plans are sketchy, often ignored, and not used because "we are experienced." Large inventories of spare parts are stored in conditions that significantly reduce their useful life. Operators ignore the early warning signs of pending failure. Furthermore, I always hear at least 10 reasons why "we can't change the way we do things around here."

What if other industries took the same path as these organizations? Take, for example, the aircraft maintenance industry. There is a high degree of discipline from the certifications of those who perform the maintenance to the suppliers of parts and materials used on the job. Procedures are very specific, and every process and step is documented. Consequently, with more than 27,000 takeoffs and landings every day in the United States, aircraft crashes due to equipment failure rarely happen. Another good example is NASCAR Winston Cup racing. The best-of-the-best in stock car racing depend on reliable equipment to do their job; every race car must meet rigid safety guidelines and has to be reliable. The old saying in the pits is; "If you can't finish, you can't win." Achieving 100 percent reliability takes discipline and teamwork. Organizations that want to compete and become "world class" need to successfully implement Total Productive Maintenance (TPM) programs.

TPM requires effective leadership from the start. That is part of the meaning of "total" in Total Productive Maintenance. Without effective leadership that links TPM efforts to the business and holds people accountable for performing highly specified work, equipment performance and reliability will continue to decline and TPM initiatives will be short-lived. Many of today's business leaders have risen through the ranks when maintenance was only responsible for "fixing things" not for preventing problems. Viewing maintenance as a non-value-adding support function, they often subject the maintenance department to severe cost-cutting; this usually results in higher costs due to decreased equipment effectiveness.

Companies that have been successful usually follow an implementation plan that includes the following 12 steps:

Step 1: Announcement of TPM. Top management needs to create an environment that will support the introduction of TPM. Without the support of management, scepticism and resistance will kill the initiative.

Step 2: Launch a formal education program. This program will inform and educate everyone in the organization about TPM activities, benefits and the importance of contribution from everyone.

Step 3: Create an organizational support structure. This group will promote and sustain TPM activities once they begin. Team-based activities are essential to a TPM effort. This group needs to include members from every level of the organization from management to the shop floor. This structure will promote communication and will guarantee everyone is working toward the same goals.

Step 4: Establish basic TPM policies and quantifiable goals. Analyze the existing conditions and set goals that are SMART: Specific, Measurable, Attainable, Realistic and Time-based.

Step 5: Outline a detailed master deployment plan. This plan will identify what resources will be needed and when for training, equipment restoration and improvements, maintenance management systems and new technologies.

Step 6: TPM kick-off. Implementation will begin at this stage.

Step 7: Improve the effectiveness of each piece of equipment. Project teams will analyze each piece of equipment and make the necessary improvements.

Step 8: Develop an autonomous maintenance program for operators. Operators' routine cleaning and inspection will help stabilize conditions and stop accelerated deterioration.

Step 9: Develop a planned or preventive maintenance program. Create a schedule for preventive maintenance on each piece of equipment.

Step 10: Conduct training to improve operation and maintenance skills. The maintenance department will take on the role of teachers and guides to provide training, advice and equipment information to the teams.

Step 11: Develop an early equipment management program. Apply preventive maintenance principles during the design process of equipment.

Step 12: Continuous improvement. As in any lean initiative, the organization needs to develop a continuous improvement mind-set.

Maintenance and reliability as a core business strategy is key to a successful TPM implementation. Without the support of top management, TPM will be just another "flavour of the month." Implementing TPM using the above 12 steps will start you on the road to "zero breakdowns" and "zero defects."

Chapter 15: Maximizing Equipment Efficiency

In today's global marketplace, opportunities and competition are the catch phrases and companies are drawing business strategies to deliver reliable products or services satisfying all customer requirements on time. The prices of the product or service must be low enough to be competitive and at the same time fetch profitable revenues for the company. It follows that manufacturing companies should focus more on the reduction and elimination of unnecessary costs associated with material and time wastages.

Thus, a great deal of attention should be paid to the reliability of production lines and their efficient functioning. Although many companies automate most of their manufacturing operations, maintenance activities depend profoundly on human inputs. As stated in earlier chapters Total Productive Maintenance (TPM) is a productive maintenance program, which focuses on:
1. Maximizing equipment effectiveness.
2. Establishing a thorough system of Preventive Maintenance (PM) for the equipment's entire life span.
3. Involving every single employee from top management to shop floor workers.
4. Empowering employees to initiate corrective activities.

Philosophically, TPM closely resembles Total Quality Management (TQM) in that many of the TQM tools like employee empowerment, benchmarking and documentation are used to implement and optimize TPM.

Bringing maintenance into the forefront; TPM focuses on scheduling it as an integral part of the manufacturing process. The goal is to minimize and eventually eliminate emergency and unscheduled maintenance by:

1. Designing and implementing improvement activities to enhance equipment efficiency.
2. Training equipment operators to be "equipment conscious", "equipment skilled" and establishing a system of autonomous maintenance to be performed by them.
3. Establishing a planned maintenance system.
4. Conducting training courses to help operators improve their skills.
5. Creating a system of Maintenance Prevention (MP) design and early equipment management. MP design generates equipment requiring minimal maintenance and early equipment management makes new equipment operational in a short time.

Obstacles

Like any other improvement initiative, implementation of TPM also has a few obstacles, crucial among them being LACK of:

1. Management support and understanding.
2. Sufficient training.

3. Time for the evolution of TPM.

Thus, successful implementation of TPM demands on commitment, structure and direction.

Key factors for successful implementation of TPM

1. Approach TPM realistically, develop a practical plan, employ program and project management principles.
2. Accept that implementation of TPM takes a longer time and change existing attitudes towards maintenance.
3. Train and deploy a network of TPM coordinators to promote and support TPM activities every day.
4. Support the TPM coordinators with time and resources and senior level backup.
5. Develop relevant measures of performance and continuously monitor and publicize benefits achieved in financial terms.
6. Be determined to keep going.

Successful TPM companies

Toyota, Harley Davidson and Texas Instruments are few of the companies that have implemented TPM successfully. All of these companies have reported 50% or greater reduction in downtime, reduced spare parts inventory and increased on-time deliveries. Texas Instruments reported 80% increased production in some areas and Toyota reported over 90% increased productivity.

Today, with business competition at an all time high, TPM may be one of the key factors that separates success and failure. If everyone involved in a TPM program works with dedication, TPM will definitely bring in high rates of return.

The goal of TPM

With TPM, the maintenance, production and engineering departments have to develop the spirit of teamwork and work towards Zero defects, Zero accidents and Zero breakdowns. In addition TPM aims to:

1. Improve the state of maintenance.
2. Improve product quality.
3. Reduce waste.
4. Reduce manufacturing costs.

TPM identifies the following crucial factors that limit the effectiveness of equipment:

1. Breakdown of equipment.
2. Set-up and adjustment downtime.
3. Idling and minor stoppages.
4. Reduced speed.
5. Process defects.
6. Reduced yield.

Conventionally, equipment failure is often given importance only when failure reaches the extent that production is stopped. In spite of recognizing potential failure conditions, production operators often continue with the process without giving the maintenance staff a chance to make adjustments and repairs, which are crucial to get the equipment working to its full potential.

The quality and the output suffer in such circumstances and this is a "waste" in terms of world-class manufacturing. TPM aims to overcome/prevent such "waste" by involving operators in reducing equipment failures during the production process or during set-up changes by:

1. Keeping work surfaces clean to prevent contamination and wear.
2. Reporting oil leakages and ensuring that action is taken to prevent recurrence in future.
3. Being alert and recognizing unusual noise, vibrations, smell and temperature which signify impending failure.
4. Checking bolts for tightness (which maintenance experts consider as the single most important cause of machine failure).
5. Reporting any deterioration in product quality before the issue goes out-of-control.
6. Studying process control charts and taking corrective action before control levels of processes are breached.

Benefits of TPM

TPM results in improved workforce skills

For this, the operators have to be trained and guided by maintenance specialists. Generally, equipment suppliers train skilled technicians in skills required to maintain the equipment supplied by them; however the advent of increasingly advanced and complex processes in manufacturing operations has necessitated the need to inculcate "multiple skills" in technicians. Many world-class companies have such skilled and trained technicians trained in their production team. In addition to the primary task of production, these technicians have the additional responsibility of monitoring the condition of the equipment as it operates. This helps to detect and rectify problems in the initial stages itself.

TPM facilitates improved relationships between operations and maintenance

1. Operators and technicians develop multiple skills, leading to job enrichment and improved flexibility of workers.
2. The involvement of operators in routine maintenance builds a sense of responsibility, ownership and pride.
3. Better co-ordination reduces delays and downtimes and productivity increases.

Total Productive Maintenance should be introduced only after the organization's culture changes to one in which the entire workforce is dedicated to improving the business. There should not be any conflicts between the various departments especially production and maintenance departments.

Total Productive Maintenance thrives on the spirit of teamwork. It has a long-range outlook and may take a year to implement. It works not only in the manufacturing industry, but also in the service industry, construction, building maintenance and a variety of other situations.

Chapter 16: Best Practices for Preventive Maintenance

In this chapter we will look at examples of best practices and the questions you need to ask to determine if your plant is using them.

Visiting plants in different corners of the world, we often are asked.

What are the current best practices for preventive maintenance (PM)?

We usually answer that we define preventive maintenance using 95 key elements. We also point out, to some people's dismay, that there is no single silver bullet for improving PM, but rather many combined efforts will be required to eventually yield results.

Here are a few key elements along with test questions and best practice (BP) examples to help you gauge how well your plant practices measure up.

Do you have a definition for preventive maintenance?

Interview test: Ask people in maintenance and operations to define what is included in preventive maintenance.

BP example: We have a definition of preventive maintenance that is documented, understood, and well communicated across our plant.

Having a definition of preventive maintenance is important for good communication in meetings, improvement efforts, and training seminars. For example, are detailed cleaning, balancing, and alignment part of preventive maintenance? Is operator inspection part of PM? Are operating practices part of PM?

We have often attended meetings or interviews where we are told a plant is continuously working on improving preventive maintenance. When we ask for the plant's definition of PM, we notice that there are as many definitions of PM as there are people. How can we expect to improve PM if we are not clear on what PM really is? We define PM as essential care and condition monitoring. Perhaps you can use the definition in your plant.

Do you know how satisfactory PM is done today?

Test: Ask the plant manager, maintenance manager, and operations manager for the PM improvement plan. If there is one, is it specific with timelines? For example: Lubrication storage improvement complete by August 2014.

BP: Plant management is aware of strengths and weaknesses of the PM program. The plant therefore has specific plans and timelines in place for improvement actions.

We interviewed people in plants to get a good idea of how well PM is done. When initially asking a person how well PM is done in their plant, the first answer is; Yes, we do this all the time. After some more discussion and specific questions around PM, the interviewee changes the statement to; Well, we probably do this most of the time. After more small talk and several cups of coffee and more explanations around PM the interviewee states; I know we definitely, sometimes do it.

The questions become more specific and the interviewee downgrades the statement to; I think we do it. Time passes and questions around, for example, alignment standards, condition monitoring routes, and operator involvement make the interviewee think of what good PM really is, and the statement is changed to; Somebody told me we did it. When we finally have defined what best practices in preventive maintenance are and there is a stack of coffee mugs, the person muses, We used to do it all the time.

By first defining what PM is, and then educating and training people in the current state of their actual PM performance, the groundwork for improvement is laid.

Do you have an alignment standard, and is it followed?

Test: Ask for an alignment standard and check quality of standard. Go to look at equipment for signs of good or poor alignment.

BP: There is a well-documented alignment standard. More importantly, the standard is followed.

In a world-class reliability and maintenance organization, all alignments are done to 0.002 in. (0.05 mm) for equipment running below 3600 rpm and 0.001 in. (0.025 mm) for equipment running above 3600 rpm. There is a well-defined alignment standard explaining how to set up, clean, check for pipe strain, check for soft foot, etc.

Take a tour of your plant. If alignment is done well there are jacking bolts (push bolts) installed on all motors, gears, and other equipment of significance. Bases and foundations are in good condition and no more than four shims are used under the motor feet. Overall vibration level is low in the plant (0.1 in./sec unfiltered average). As a tracking indicator, see if alignment records are kept for each alignment job.

Do you have a lubrication standard, and is it followed?

Test: The standard should include storage, handling, filtering, and cleanliness of lubricants. Visually check cleanliness of storage areas and handling.

BP: There is a well-documented lubrication standard. More importantly, the standard is followed.

The cleanliness standard for each piece of equipment should match the clearances in the equipment's lubricated surfaces. For example, a hydraulic unit may need to be filtered down to 3 microns (200 beta) and a gearbox to 12 microns (75 beta).

In order to reach the right cleanliness levels of lubricants, oil and grease have to be stored, handled, and filtered correctly. Few people know that new oil usually is delivered at around 40 microns cleanliness level, which means that oil going into equipment with fine clearances should be filtered.

Are inspections (condition monitoring) done where it is cost effective to do so?

Test: Go through inspection lists, check for level of detail, and make sure the route is actually completed.

BP: There are inspection routes for all mechanical, electrical, and instrumentation equipment (where it is cost effective to have inspections).

In a top-notch plant, inspections are documented and completed according to schedule. The plant is using an inspection list or, even better, a handheld computer. The list or handheld computer describes exactly what to do for each inspection. The inspections are a combination of measuring condition and subjective (look, listen, feel, smell) inspections.

Most inspections are completed while equipment is operating because we do not want to waste valuable shutdown/offline time on inspections that could be done on the run. Inspections can usually be done better when equipment is operating. For example, a pump cannot really be inspected well when it is down since there are no vibration, no operating pressures, and no seal water flow.

To see if your plant is performing according to world-class reliability and maintenance standards, take an inspection list, or handheld computer (if you do not have inspection lists, it is time to develop them), and walk the route. For example, check the following:

1. Do we have condition monitoring routes covering all necessary inspections?
2. Do we use simple inspection tools such as a stroboscope, infrared thermometer, vibration pen, industrial stethoscope, bright flashlights (500,000 candela), and inspection mirrors?
3. Can we inspect couplings, belts, and chains on the run, or do guards make it impossible?
4. Are inspections being done? Are oil glasses clean enough to see oil levels, are base bolts clean enough to check tightness etc.?
5. Are people educated and trained in basic inspection techniques?

Is detailed cleaning of equipment done well?

Test: Take a walk in your plant and visually check the cleanliness and condition of the equipment.

BP: Detailed cleaning of equipment is done consistently. Dirty areas are redesigned in order to protect equipment from contamination.

Detailed cleaning can be checked easily. For example, a clean hydraulic unit can be inspected for leaks in about 10 sec by taking a quick look at the pan underneath the unit. A dirty hydraulic unit would take 20-30 minutes to check for leaks.

Is an ultrasonic or vibration monitor used when greasing bearings?

Test: Check lubricator's equipment.

BP: Vibration or ultrasonic levels (or other method) are checked while greasing in order to apply the correct amount of grease.

Greasing is done by measuring ultrasonic or vibration levels while applying grease to the bearing. It is almost impossible to know how much grease is applied to a bearing without a measurement. The measurement tools indicate to us when the grease hits the bearings and monitor the vibration or ultrasonic levels as grease is squeezed into the bearing. Over and under greasing can be avoided by using the right tools. An alternate method is to use a volume meter, assuming the required grease volume for the bearing is known.

Although just a sample of the 95 points we use to evaluate plant performance, these example tests and best practices demonstrate the methodology by which one can build a system for discussing performance levels.

More Questions and Answers

Question: I have heard the term TPM (Total Productive Maintenance) as being the "best practice" for maintaining equipment. Can you help me understand what it is and how it differs from regular maintenance?

Answer: Over the past few decades there has been reactive, preventative and predictive maintenance. Each offered advantages over its predecessor. This is also true of total productive maintenance.

Total productive maintenance consists of the integration the concept of lean manufacturing into the manufacturing process.

It is common in many companies to charge employees with taking care of the lubrication needs for several pieces of equipment. It is also common that work requiring a tool requires a maintenance person to perform it. If there is a problem with a photo cell or controls, an electrician would be required.

Under the TPM philosophy, any of the work the operator is capable of and this varies by individual; would be done by the operator; he or she would not have to wait for a different employee to come and fix the problem. Along with these activities, the operators are also responsible for the cleanliness and organization of their work area.

The TPM philosophy consists of three major components. These are:
1. Teamwork approach to increase Operational Equipment Efficiency (OEE).
2. Eliminating waste from the process of maintaining the equipment.

3. Improve the ownership/moral of the machine operators.

There are specific practices embedded in these components. The major practices are:
1. Autonomous maintenance (the equipment operator does much of the maintenance).
2. The practice of 5S (Sort, Set in order, Shine, Standardize and Sustain).
3. Planning all maintenance activities.
4. Technical training.

The benefits of TPM are directly related to the way you perform your maintenance today. TPM has many quantifiable advantages for many companies around the world, but it is only a benefit if it moves your organization forward. If you find you do not have the barriers that TPM is designed to overcome, no problem; just wait for condition based maintenance.

Source: (Torbjörn Idhammar President, IDCON INC) www.idcon.com

Chapter 17: Asset Management Strategy

With the right asset management strategy, you could be on a path to exceed your productivity targets and sustain continued growth and competitiveness.

Does this sound familiar? You have a failure on your plant so your team tries to either track you down, an OEM engineer or the systems integrator that put the system in few years ago. The clock is ticking and production is at a standstill while you try to determine the fault. If a part is needed, you chase around to get repair bids, issue POs and deal with invoices and you face the same challenges to get an engineer on site.

Why does it have to be so complicated?

Most company arrive at this situation by accident rather than design and in an ideal world we might design something like this.

1. Evaluate needs and set goals

Examine your current situation while keeping in mind your business priorities. Identify critical areas of concern and opportunities for improvement to build a vision of what success looks like using the following elements.

  a. Determine criticality of process stages by assessing equipment priority and risks.

b. Identify serviceable equipment components with their lifecycle status (available, repairable, replaceable or obsolete).

c. Storeroom contents and all other locations holding spares.

2. Design and implement your strategy

What you determine during goal-setting will become the foundation for your maintenance process and may include.

a. **Storeroom Management:** Placement and content of the central and distributed stores, ensuring layout and design provides easy access for frequently required parts. Employ an intelligent numbering, labelling and tracking solution to allow an SKU rationalisation assessment.

b. **Inventory Management:** Parts reduction is a popular target as it frees up cash, but it may conflict with critical parts availability. Ideally remove or 'burn off' excess inventory and build up stock where you have gaps in critical spares. Work with your local distributor to stock some of your needed parts and collaborate with your equipment vendor to implement an on-site parts management solution.

c. **Process Management:** Implement parts tracking procedure to assess each component's lifecycle. Document where, when and why they fail, determine if they are under warranty and track when they are sent for repair.

d. **Reporting and Dashboards:** Using an OEE approach can illustrate uptime trending and downtime due to component failure, as well as showing a strong financial return.

e. **Migration Projects:** If your facility is more than 10 years old, your machine risk assessment and spare parts availability will tell you where migration projects are required. Rank these for future capital spending and tackle critical migrations immediately. Mitigate risks by working with your vendors to guarantee reserve spares.

f. **Preventative maintenance:** Look for solutions from vendors such as scheduled service visits, fully warranted replacement parts or remote web monitoring for troubleshooting.

3. Measure and optimise

Consider the installed base asset register a living document by adjusting it as new equipment is installed and old is scrapped. Use the information gathered to turn into actionable, prioritised decisions. Sharing this data with your suppliers helps to hold them accountable, as well as giving them the data and opportunity to support you better.

Benefits

Good asset management can assist in not only reducing costs and inefficiencies; ultimately it can improve production uptime and increase productivity, allowing you to.

1. Minimise downtime by ensuring spares are easily accessible, identifying the right spares for critical equipment.
2. Reduce costs through SKU rationalisation, removing parts for obsolete equipment and burning off excess spares.
3. Ensure warranties are used and failures tracked to make appropriate decisions on new replacement or repairs.
4. Achieve savings by tracking parts and component failures by machine, line and shift, to identify candidates for machine adjustment or perhaps migration.

While best practice asset management is logical, day-to-day pressures often get in the way. Outsourcing asset management to a trusted source allows you to focus on the preventative and visionary activities.

Chapter 18: Operators Involvement in Maintenance

Why waste the skills and first-hand knowledge of operators?

I've got a 44-year-old Morris Minor for dry days and hill-free roads. I know every sound and vibration that Mungo makes. I know the difference between the rattling quiver that says his trunnions need greasing and the deeper clunk-shake that says I should have got new ones last week. I am Mungo's driver, not his mechanic; but he spends less time in the workshop because I can spot the early signs of problems!

It's no different on the factory floor; the person who best understands the machine is the person who operates or drives it. Breakdowns are often averted because an operator has told the duty engineer that it doesn't sound right today. Many factories save hours of expensive craft time when operators who really know their machines take over frontline tasks such as cleaning, lubricating and replacing filters.

So, surely operator involvement in maintenance should be a given in most plants?

Not according to recent research a friend of mine carried out. Some 40% of sites think their operators only moderately understand their plant, while 45% have no formal maintenance training programme. Yet there is no doubt that many plant managers have real worries about the future of their maintenance operations; fears about an ageing workforce or over-dependence upon external contractors (91% outsource some or all of their maintenance) are common across the board.

Deeper operator involvement is an obvious solution to both current and future problems. Reality, however, is very different to theory.

The absence of a workable strategy is often costing manufacturers far more than they realise. The same issues is always cropping up in so many factories. Management has cut back numbers and installed more automation in the name of efficiency. They may even believe they have put a strategy in place to extend the operators' role to replacing parts, handling changeovers and set-ups. But their training processes have been cursory, in reality equipping them to do little more than a push-button fulfilment of the basics. As a result, experienced craftsmen get pulled in as super-setters which, in turn, means that important maintenance tasks don't get done.

This engineering/production divide is not so pronounced in sectors like chemicals, brewing and distilling, where there is a higher calibre of operator who tends to understand the controlling parameters of the equipment; but in food and drink, we often see the results of expediency. Getting people is not easy and seasonal peaks make things worse through hiring temporary labour. So it makes the demand for hand-holding by the craft technicians even higher. They are spending up to half their time on it; time that otherwise could be used in maintaining and improving and the irony is that the lost time and production is booked as engineering downtime. There is a belief that, because the solution came through the engineers, engineering must be the root cause of the problem; but it's not engineering that's broke; it's the skills and the processes behind the way the operators work.

Even sites that understand and value the role of maintenance often fail to involve their operators successfully. Our research, among sites using asset management improvement service audited as a benchmark, showed that a large percentage had tried autonomous maintenance and failed.

Autonomous maintenance is an essential ingredient of TPM (total productive maintenance), the gold standard of resource management, with responsibility firmly shared between production and maintenance. Through the work of lean improvement teams, maintenance activity steadily moves away from reactive to preventive/predictive work, bringing stability to the entire planning process.

It incorporates technical disciplines such as RCM (reliability centred maintenance), a process to establish the safe minimum levels of maintenance needed to ensure that assets continue to perform as needed.

TPM is an all-pervading philosophy that put into action through the appropriate techniques; tunes the entire manufacturing environment to peak performance; but TPM is also a daunting challenge; it affects every aspect of the manufacturing and support operations. Many organisations, with some justice, doubt their own ability to see it through. So they have got a straight choice; find someone to help them through it or adopt a less taxing approach that will still bring some, although not all, of the advantages.

There are, of course, a number of good consultancies that specialise in TPM support. Bearing in mind, however, the growing trend for outsourcing, it is interesting to see how the work of a third party maintenance company can be effectively dovetailed with an operator engagement programme.

Golden rules for asset care
1. Don't even start making changes until you are sure you have overcome the barrier of I break, you fix. Operators need to feel motivated to share responsibility for machine condition and performance.
2. Do not assume that the operator knows what is needed. Invest the time to train and get the buy-in of operators and supervisors.
3. Managers should establish a framework to solicit operators opinions and support their new activities. Feed their observations into the planned maintenance checklists and acknowledge their contribution.
4. Managers should choose a pilot that has challenges but also the potential for rapid gains. Make sure that all shifts participate and promote the successes across the business.

Chapter 19: Tight Cost Controls

Tight cost controls mean manufacturers are turning to employees rather than new equipment to maximise productivity.

Manufacturers are ramping up workforce skills and moral to combat productivity drains inflicted by ageing equipment, supply chain chaos and a void in talented new recruits.

Nearly three quarters of businesses are up-skilling existing staff with widespread investment in formal training and appraisal schemes.

The commitment to people power comes as firms get cold feet over splashing out on new machinery in the face of ongoing economic uncertainty.

The make-do-and-mend approach means machine downtime is proving the biggest threat to workforce productivity levels, the survey of over 150 factory managers reported. Ageing equipment is a dominant concern for maintaining future efficiencies and with cost control named the overwhelming priority in keeping that productivity up, maintenance departments might want to rethink their holiday plans.

Site managers may also want to avoid long haul destinations should they manage a summer escape. Production lines have felt the pinch of events in far. The Japan earthquake saw automotive giants enforce shutdowns at UK plants. The Libya conflict and unrest in the Middle East have resulted in spiralling oil prices and a knock-on hike in transport and energy costs for UK and US firms.

An overwhelming 61% of site managers said rising materials and energy costs were the top threat to future productivity; however, it's not just oil prices that are soaring. The mood among factory floor workers remains high despite the gathering storm. Few businesses report issues around low moral. Employees appear to be delivering a rapid return on investment for firms who have invested in staff development and training.

Much of the labour is being performed by longstanding employees who can't work forever. Businesses claim the quality of replacements coming through is not up to scratch. A toxic skills gap edges ever closer.

Staff performance soars as employers invest in people power

Take care of your staff and they will take care of you. Employers investing in a raft of formal staff training and development. In return, employees are more reliable, punctual and motivated than ever. Relations have been further buoyed by a brighter business outlook. The number of firms reporting redundancies and pay freezes has halved since June 2010. Pay rises are almost twice as common as one year ago, with 52% of businesses giving an increase compared to 30% in 2010.

Over 80% of manufacturers are running formal staff appraisal schemes. The majority of employers offer support for engineering degree and apprenticeships.

Cost control puts the strain on machinery

Manufacturers are taking a hit from misfiring machinery rather than commit to expensive upgrades while the strength of the recovery remains in doubt.

Cost control is a runaway priority for firms looking to maintain day-to-day productivity; but businesses are being left in a catch-22 scenario with the biggest slumps in shop floor efficiency being blamed on equipment downtime.

Manufacturers told us that they would continue to patch up plant wherever possible rather than re-equip because of fears over long-term business demand. Factory managers cited rising energy costs as the biggest risk to future productivity, but ageing equipment and capital budget equipment restrictions both featured in the top three of our findings.

Chapter 20: TPM Strategy Deployment

Total productive maintenance (TPM) can make a huge difference; not only in terms of machine uptime, but also in shop floor engagement.

TPM has been a key enabler for this business, says General Manager at a steel manufacturing company. His 130 plus employee plant, in the UK takes steel coil, which it slits and processes for others to then use. The site has a number of large slitting machines that have benefited from the maintenance regime, as well as a lot of materials handling equipment; substantial-sized cranes, as well as forklift trucks and more.

The General Manager doesn't claim to be an expert on TPM, but the story of its introduction at the site is interesting. "We are a business that has tried to step up to the lean challenge," he explains," and gradually we have realised that TPM is an integral part of that." Three years ago, however, when he moved to this site, that realisation had yet to dawn. "By pushing forward with other lean approaches, we have been forced to get to grips with TPM." he said.

The site has worked hard in a number of areas such as safety, continuous improvement, productivity, SMED and 5S, to name but a few and the business has found that TPM is not only an integral part of all these; it is, in fact, essential. Despite this, he has deliberately chosen not to brand the technique as TPM. "You can get operator fatigue from initiative overload," he says.

One area where TPM has helped, not surprisingly, is safety. In the past, the lost time accident frequency rate (LTAFR) was 17, he said; "Now, however, we haven't had an accident; we have totally changed the culture."

How did TPM help? Take cranes, for example. "We realised that preventative maintenance is an integral part of safety," he said. "Until you spend time on TPM, you are not going to engineer out safety problems." For the cranes, much analysis was carried out to understand how the equipment was performing and all the cranes are now managed via TPM. "We do time-based maintenance, usage-based maintenance, track all movements, monitor the kit... and all this is done as a matter of routine. "He is convinced that the only way to ensure maximum safety and productivity for the crane operations is with TPM.

Remember, however, that he has not branded it TPM. "What we've done is establish a very deliberate path, starting with strategy deployment." A strategy was generated and communicated, with specific information given to the employees. What is more, this was all deployed visually. This embraced a good deal of the basics, such as 5S, but he built TPM into everything and it's not only safety that benefits. "5S and SMED are inherently TPM territory," he points out.

Another interesting aspect has been the impact on the shop floor. Despite having what he describes as a great maintenance department, "we had an issue with the culture here, where operators didn't even bother reporting faults". It seems work was planned, prioritised, then carried out; but as the operators didn't see this straight away, they didn't believe things were actually happening. "Operators felt that they had no impact on maintenance," he explains.

Now fault lists, wish lists - even 'what would you like your machine to look like' are all documented by the operators on the machines. The fault reporting system changed radically. Now, when a repair is carried out, the person who raised the fault must sign it off to say they are happy with the work. "It becomes a virtuous circle," he said.

Notably, this has resulted in autonomous maintenance being taken away from the operators. Daily inspections were being performed, but the system as a whole wasn't working. "So we've brought inspections back within the remit of maintenance," he said. The result? "Clarity of roles." He admits this approach wouldn't work for every business, but he advises trying different strategies before deciding whether they are appropriate. It certainly worked in this case.

In addition to the massive improvement in safety at the site, productivity has increased by 35% in 12 months. He is in no doubt that the use of TPM albeit "behind the scenes" has been the driver for this. Even without the branding, TPM still supports all improvement efforts at the plant. "Operators wouldn't necessarily say this, but I know it is. Our maintenance approach now has a professional edge."

This is a great example of the importance of TPM, but there are some key points for everyone; leadership, measurement, systems and, of course, doing what is right for your business.

The success of TPM, like most elements of world-class manufacturing, consists of 10% technical knowledge, 20% strategic context and 70% management commitment and leadership.

Part of the leader's role is to educate. Adults simply do not respond well to being told what to do, without learning for themselves why. Too few Operation Directors (VP Operations) have been exposed to the concepts of adult education to understand the fundamental need to enable engineers, operators and supervisors to jointly study, discuss, modify and maintain operating assets together.

If your business is one where engineers are summoned, grumbling from their hidey-hole to fix machinery under the blank gaze of an on looking operator, while being berated by the shift supervisor for being useless, lazy and/or slow, you know that you not they are at fault. If this sounds depressingly familiar, fear not. It's simple to break this cycle. The TPM cocktail requires one strong leader, a real business need, a simple framework to work within and a well balanced blend of operators, engineers and supervision. Depending on your taste, your ingredients can be shaken or stirred prior to serving.

At the end of the day, who is running the hen house?

Management must manage the change. That is the challenge. A problem exists with the image of maintenance, though. It has never been sexy. Typically, you don't find a 'VP of Maintenance' for example, we did a study with a company in the UK to find out about asset management strategies. Some 93% said that asset management was important, but less than 30% have senior management involved in that piece of the business.

Maintenance is fairly simple. If you focus on a few key items, you can have dramatic results. These results can be seen through good measures. How many are really measuring it? Two thirds of PMs never get done. If you measure it, you reap the results.

You get what you measure; so 30% compliance can go up to 60% or 70% compliance.

One side of TPM that can be missed is that operational and maintenance people may want new tools to help them plan and measure, but may not be able to articulate what they need, in terms of value.

Chapter 21: Using TPM to Gain Stable Position

Is it total productive maintenance or total predictive maintenance, or even as belated recognition that its impact goes way beyond the engineering department total productive manufacturing? Too many words for something straightforward; a way to stop wasting your time fixing machines when you could be making good products. TPM however you choose to spell it out is absolutely fundamental to the operations of any company claiming lean working or pursuing world-class manufacturing.

Within lean, the most obvious implementation of TPM principles is autonomous maintenance, where operators take responsibility for basic first-line maintenance. Without good planned preventative maintenance (PM) from the engineers, it won't work. Yet, many lean implementations often ignore the role of the maintenance department completely for example three similarly sized medical device manufacturers we use to work with gained from lean a significant some of $3.6m across the three plants; but $1.5m of that is actually attributable to maintenance activities through improved asset care and even that ignores the net effect of the maintenance department's engineering and process improvement skills in reducing defects and levels of intervention. That stacks up to a hefty $917,000 coming directly from process optimisation and more than doubles the contribution made by maintenance to total lean gains.

It gets worse. Maintenance leaders from 50 major manufacturers were surveyed to find out what impact they could have on the seven lean wastes. The average score was 51 out of a possible 63 (showing significant impact across all areas). Yet not one of their companies had initiated a programme that directly engaged the maintenance function in supporting lean manufacturing processes. I wonder if the engineers bothered to hide their resentment?

We could blames the pioneers of lean who formulated their approach by observing Japanese lean methods. The Japanese already knew and valued the importance of equipment reliability. For those observing a reliable flow process, however, it was a bit like looking at a building and not realising how deep its foundations are; they could see operators doing maintenance. What they couldn't see was that it was only one element of what's needed.

Let's look at how one plant has adapted TPM to support its own production process. The consumables plant of a High Tech company based in the US, started its TPM project in 2010. The company's maintenance supervisor, was adamant that he wanted to make the whole thing modular, using the minimum amount of people to make small-scale achievements and then mapping those across to other machines and lines. It's easy for TPM to take over everything but, without any obvious, short-term gains, the whole thing often falters. He, however, planned to complete the initial programme in only nine months.

His aim was an effective, production-driven maintenance plan that would alongside the normal benefits also begin to develop operators' skills in asset care. His long-term goal is TPM across the factory.

He said to do that, you have got to benchmark improvements as you go along. It's important; it makes people want to join in. He had experienced the formal, top-down approach to TPM when he worked for another High-tech Company and believes that it hasn't really advanced since the 70s. He was keen to incorporate elements of lean and Six Sigma to combine the best of all three disciplines.

The General Manager operations, became a firm and enthusiastic backer virtually as soon as the maintenance supervisor presented the case, partly because the project clearly offered tangible gains for limited investment. "It was 2010. We were in recession and no one in manufacturing knew how they would come out at the other end. So projects like this had their merit," he recalls. The balance of his team was equally important; the company's senior technician had over 10 years' experience of TPM and the equipment engineer, had led equipment improvement for 15 years. They had the skills to drive short-term improvements in existing machines into longer-term gains through modifying and redesigning processes.

He boiled down the seven principles of classic TPM into a simple five-step plan; examine the initial condition of equipment and maintenance procedures; restore equipment to base condition; improve; simplify activities; and, finally, sustain. They started on one of the lines which had the worst downtime record, defining a method for operators to record stops and failures.

What followed was hard work without the option of delegation. The three men cleaned every bit of equipment themselves. It took them 8 hours over a weekend and with typical thoroughness.

Regular monitoring gave them the basis for an autonomous maintenance schedule. The results weren't exactly comforting because of the high level of contamination by powder, the schedule demanded roughly five hours a week offline; an actual increase over current downtime. "We couldn't lose that amount of production time so we decided to share the work in the first instance," he explained. Operators spent 35 minutes on things like nozzle cleaning while the technicians handled the bulk of the work offline.

Even at this stage there were clear benefits. Downtime was reduced to 78 minutes a week, including operators' cleaning time. Obviously, technicians were taking up some of the load but it let them inspect key parts for early signs of failure, using the results to modify and refine the existing PM schedule. The schedule was stable within only a month. With less unplanned stoppages, overtime was almost completely eliminated and the whole appearance of the place was better, both for visitors and those working there.

"The hard part in our first project is justifying it to production why we want to close the machine down. We are fortunate here that they trusted us to deliver something beneficial," he recalled. "And it's a lot easier to get buy-in on a small-scale project like this. It helped that we got a lot of things right first time which made it more appealing to management and allowed us to continue with other machines and areas of the business. Now we've seen such dramatic improvements other areas are asking for it."

Focus on detail

With stability achieved, the team turned their attention to continuous improvement. They looked at the standard lean technique of single minute exchange of dies (SMED) but decided it was better attacked separately: "It took us down a road that wouldn't be very visible to management or operators and it would increase the project time while possibly losing focus." Instead, they conducted a failure modes and effects analysis (FMEA) on the problem areas previously highlighted.

The fundamental cause of many of them was quite simply powder being deposited where it shouldn't. When pucks stopped hard, powder flew out, so they found a mechanism for softening stops to dampen impact. They introduced localised extraction at key points on the line; at the filling nozzles and the welding stage. It cost remarkably little; they spliced into an existing system.

Pucks would collide when there was a slight build up on the line, creating a powder cloud. So they designed puck-to-puck dampeners. The remarkable thing is that they did it all themselves for a tiny cost. Yet the soft-stops alone took 22.5 hours per month out of the maintenance load and, as a welcome by-product, dampening collisions cut noise levels so effectively that operators could now work without ear defenders.

FMEA threw up one major issue; filling accuracy. Each product manufacture on the line is filled to a given tolerance. The existing procedure did not account for variances in plastics and cavity types. It meant that under-filled products were regularly scrapped later in the process. Using a process capability index, the old nozzles were found to be incapable of matching the company's tolerances repeatedly. So they designed a new nozzle and sourced a firm to make them.

The company used TPM to get to a stable position where it could start using more sophisticated techniques derived from Six Sigma. It let the business clear away the simple but costly causes of production loss so it could concentrate on the underlying issues and the net beneficiary was the bottom line.

By this time, the team had designed out large chunks of the maintenance load. The basic cleaning schedule had gone from 25 hours a month to 2.5 almost immediately and much of it could be transferred to the operators for autonomous maintenance. He says they were fortunate; as with so many Japanese manufacturers, continuous improvement was already embedded in the ethos of the company and the transfer was simple. In a parallel project, they taught operators to start up the line. Rather than one technician handling it all, five operators now perform start-up checks.

Chapter 22: TPM and Culture Change

Let's face it, we all face tough challenges. Competitive pressures continue unabated. Prices are too low, and costs are too high. Companies strive to reduce costs. Some look to improve technology. Some reduce headcount. Too few have become operationally excellent.

Costs pile up in the form of defects and waste. Consider these all-too-familiar situations.
1. Output does not meet its potential due to crew-to-crew variations.
2. Utilization suffers because product changeovers take too long.
3. An important part cannot be found, so another is rushed in.

Companies attempt to improve through Lean, Six Sigma, or Total Productive Maintenance initiatives; however, studies since 1998 report that two-thirds of these initiatives fail to meet the expectations of company leaders. Learning about the methods isn't the challenge, putting them into daily practice is, as evident in these situations.
1. Process improvements often backslide.
2. Continuous improvement is just a phrase.
3. The methods of the initiative aren't institutionalized.

The root of these failings is the inability to achieve culture change. Our survey reinforced this conclusion when it found that significant culture change remains the top challenge in over 80% of the companies surveyed.

One Answer is 5S

Some companies beat the odds and foster strong, positive cultures. Danaher and Toyota are two of the better known examples.

The method of 5S is one way to engage people and contribute to culture change. 5S is a visually-oriented system of cleanliness, organization, and arrangement designed to facilitate greater productivity, safety, and quality. It engages all employees and is a foundation for more self-discipline on the job for better work and better products.

5S is visual

5S is a foundation for more disciplined actions. If workers cannot even put a tool back in its designated location, will they follow standards for production? Its visual nature makes things that are out of place stick out like a sore thumb. When properly supported, it builds a culture of continuous improvement.

The benefits of 5S are:
1. Cleaner and safer work areas: When work area is clean and organized tripping hazards and other dangers are eliminated.

2. Less wasted time through more workplace organization: When tools and materials are accessible and orderly, workers need less time to "go get" and less time to search.

3. Less space: When unneeded items are eliminated and the needed ones are organized, required floor space is dramatically reduced.

4. Improved self-discipline: The 5S system, especially its visual nature, makes abnormal conditions noticeable and makes ignoring standards more difficult.

5. Improved culture: When 5S is applied systematically, it fosters better teamwork and enthusiasm.

People like to work in a well-organized and clean environment. They feel better about themselves and better about their work, and they restore the self-discipline that is found in winning teams.

What are the 5S's?

Sorting: Separating the needed from the unneeded. Sorting activities aim to eliminate unneeded items from the work area and to perform an initial cleaning.

Simplifying: A place for everything and everything in its place, clean and ready for use. Simplifying arranges the workplace to ensure safety and efficiency.

Systematic Cleaning: Cleaning for inspection. Systematic daily cleaning and inspection of work areas and equipment help you understand current conditions and determine if corrective action is required.

Standardizing: Developing common methods for consistency. Standardizing aims to make abnormal conditions noticeable and to document agreements to ensure consistency and sustainability.

Sustaining: Holding the gains and improving. Sustaining is aimed at maintaining the improvements from the other 5S activities and improving further.

Implementing 5S

Often, companies mistakenly view 5S as a housekeeping activity. Housekeeping is housekeeping, not 5S. 5S is a visual system and a system for engaging employees. 5S must be a team effort and the results must enable anyone to "tell at a glance" what is right and what is out of place. It also must make doing the work easier. Implementing 5S occurs in two phases: initial implementation and later refinement.

Since organizing is a key to 5S, eliminating unneeded items comes first. It is wasteful to find a home for something that is not needed.

Sorting: Sorting clears the deck for the remaining activities. It can often take weeks to accomplish in any given area or department.

The steps of sorting are:
1. Establish criteria for what is not needed. For example, if something hasn't been used for a year, it may be a candidate for disposal.
2. Identify the unneeded items and move to a holding area.
3. Dispose of the not needed items, either by transferring to a department that needs them, selling them, or discarding them.
4. Conduct an initial cleaning.

Once the initial sorting is completed, the natural sequence is to get the work area organized. Simplifying, systematic cleaning, and standardizing go hand-in hand. Simply simplifying - organizing the work - area will deteriorate if the standards are not set. The next paragraphs cover each "S" separately, but they work as a system, and must be performed at the same time, or nearly so.

Simplifying: Simplifying finds a home for everything. The home should be where the item will most efficiently be stored. Frequently-used items must be as close to where they are used as possible.

The steps of simplifying are:
1. Determine a location for each item based on frequency of use and proper safety zone (decreasing the likelihood of strain injuries, for example).
2. Develop shadow boards and label items - a home for everything.
3. Determine how to replenish supplies.

4. Document layout, equipment, supplies, and agreements for returning items to their homes.

Systematic Cleaning: Systematic cleaning provides a way to inspect, by doing a clean sweep around a work area. This means visually as well as with a broom or rags. The idea is make the job of doing daily cleaning and inspections easier.

The steps of systematic cleaning are:
1. Identify points to check for performance.
2. Determine acceptable performance.
3. Mark equipment and controls with visual indicators (e.g., gauges show the correct range).
4. Conduct daily cleaning and visual checks.

Standardizing: Standardizing assures that everyone knows what is expected. Since the workplace team establishes the standards, everyone should have had some involvement in establishing the 5S in their work area. Still, it is important to make these standards very clear.

The steps in standardizing are:
1. Establish a routine check sheet for each work area. The check sheet is like a pilot's pre-flight check list. It shows what the team should check during self-audits.
2. Establish a multi-level audit system where each level in the organization has a role to play in ensuring that 5S is sustained in the

work areas and that the 5S system evolves and strengthens.

3. Establish and document standard methods across similar work areas.
4. Document any new standard methods for doing the work.

Sustaining: Sustaining is usually thought of as the toughest "S." however, it doesn't need to be. The trick is to let the 5S system work for you. When you get to this point, you should have engaged everyone in the work area during 5S activities and have a "tell at a glance" visual workplace. If this is so, then sustaining is much easier. That is important, but not sufficient. A more systematic way to prevent backsliding and to foster continuous improvement is needed.

The steps of sustaining are:
1. Determine the 5S level of achievement - the overall grade.
2. Perform worker-led routine 5S checks using the 5S check list.
3. Address backsliding and new opportunities found during routine checks.
4. Conduct scheduled, routine checks by team leads or supervisors or by people from outside of the workgroup.
5. Perform higher-level audits to evaluate how well the 5S system is working overall. For example, are there systemic issues with sustaining 5S? Often, the company's safety committee is an excellent body for conducting these audits.

It is through sustaining activities that the practice of 5S is refined. When items aren't returned to their homes, the cause is most likely to be that the home was inconvenient. When the work team addresses these problems, they improve the sustainability of 5S and, more importantly, they improve safety, moral, and productivity.

Although 5S will not solve all of today's competitive challenges, it does provide a solid foundation for achieving operational excellence. In fact, some world-class companies claim that there can be no improvement without 5S.

The teamwork and discipline built through 5S improve worker-to-worker and worker-to-manager relationships. When people see that what they do makes a difference, and when they see that they have eliminated wasteful practices, their pride grows. This is perhaps the greatest benefit of 5S.

Chapter 23: Embedding TPM into Business

Embedding TPM into the business can be a slow journey, but how long does it take to make it pay? As one of the companies we work with discovers, less time than you think if you get your priorities right.

There is a widespread perception that TPM (total productive maintenance) is a long slog that turns your hair grey and only shows real, measurable results after three years or more. As a result, a lot of businesses never finish what they started. We believe any business satisfied with that rate of progress will get as little as it deserves.

Expectations are often pitched lower than they ought to be because TPM is often seen merely as operator or autonomous maintenance; only 20% of the TPM toolkit and something that doesn't deliver much benefit on its own. You also need to raise planned maintenance standards and the quality of education and training to support any transfer of routine activities from maintenance to production.

In addition, to get a payback from TPM, the focus should be improving overall equipment effectiveness (OEE). This requires leadership and direction to convert the capacity created through improved OEE into business benefits because typically that means changing management and maintenance roles.

We ran a four-day TPM workshop for a major Medical Device company which generated $200,000 in added value by day three. It cost less than $4,000, creating a payback of around one week. We admits this sort of rate of return is unusual but points to a recent programme in part of a major FTSE 100 company to incorporate TPM within its Lean Sigma continuous improvement (CI) process. It led to a 10% increase in OEE and therefore increase capacity in around one month. Typically those organisations which do it right produce an increase in capacity of around 50% over three years. Assuming a gross margin of 50%, that is an increase in net profits of between 50 and 200%, depending on whether you can sell the additional capacity. One of the major paybacks from TPM is the management and specialist time released from fire fighting and frontline problem solving. If this time is reinvested in proactive business improvement, the payback is measured in months if not days.

We paints a very attractive picture above but how easy is it to achieve steady, incremental gains in practice?

Impossible if you don't start right. Any move into TPM has to be seen as compatible with and integrated into the normal way of working. There is a parallel between poor adoptions of 5S and TPM. People go through the motions but don't get why they are doing it. TPM is not the end goal; it's merely a tool to support you in reaching a business objective. The TPM programmes that are working are those with a clear link between the activities taking place and the results being delivered. But if people see it as a maintenance or equipment related thing, rather than engaging all functions, you will never get the best out of it. We would warn anyone embarking on TPM that you need a reason to change. If you are just doing it because you think it's the thing to do, it isn't going to last and the key to progressing both TPM and lean is the engagement, involvement and accountability of the workforce. If you try to push in new tools and techniques without having them on board, you are equally destined to fail. Similarly, we are adamant that it is pointless jumping into planned maintenance if the place is filthy and hasn't got the discipline of 5S. "Orderliness, engagement and all the other 5S principles are essential. Sometimes people jump into the complex without getting the simple, basic things right. If you get those right, the complex things will fall into place almost by themselves.

Although he believes that everyone must understand they are in for the long haul, tangible early successes are essential. Focus on the vital few; the things that are going to give you the biggest payback and the quick wins. It grabs hearts and minds in the senior stakeholders and the board, and gets buy-in if you need investment. The philosophy is a journey that may take years but within that you can still get some really quick, important paybacks.

Let's look at one of the companies we work with approach to TPM in more detail. When the Operations Manager joined; the company already had the lean foundations securely in place. The workforce had also been trained in TPM but it was not yet embedded in their daily routines and behaviour.

The shop floor works in cell-based teams with no separate engineering and production staff. The Operations Manager's very straightforward approach centres on up-skilling the workforce and simplifying the equipment. He carries fundamental lean principles like visual management into TPM, making remedial actions obvious and foolproof; like a plug that will only go in one way so it doesn't take highly skilled engineers to handle the majority of the work. He also brought the workforce's skill level up through education. Where there is ownership, accountability and engagement, one do not need separate team. We admits that sometimes they get caught out and it means calling in extra expertise; but that's an opportunity to find out what you need to do to prevent it ever happening again. It's driving change all the way through the same principle that works in kaizen and Continuous Improvement. Our other mandatory requirement for TPM is a good assessment process. We are wholehearted believer that what gets measured gets done. Each area of the factory measures its current state of ownership and involvement, OEE, current condition, equipment care, problem prevention measures and their effectiveness. They then develop their own 18-24 month roadmap of where they are going and how. The local manager sets the targets for achieving it and the Operation's Manager reviews it with them quarterly.

You have a key stake in the ground and measures, with KPIs set against your enablers and your process to drive performance. Instead of things being done on an ad hoc basis, the measurement cycle provides a structured approach for focusing on the priorities. The detailed information is invaluable for pinpointing the bottleneck processes and therefore the quick wins.

Once you have won the hearts and minds by making a real difference to the bottlenecks, that sense of engagement will go across the whole business. Put simply, bottlenecks impede the ability to meet any growth in demand. By improving machine performance, equipment runs for longer, output is increased and more likely to be right first time and thus the business can sell all it makes. In the first year of TPM, The company took OEE in a key extrusion process from 69% to 74%. That realise $100,000 on the bottom line and it doesn't take a great investment to do it. Some of it is really low-hanging fruit.

Each target for improvement is then broken down into small, bite-sized chunks with the full involvement of the cell team. The team leader is tasked to be responsible for each team's delivery of a minimum of six improvements from 15 shift teams in the first year. Last year that stacked up to a hefty 137 improvements across the site; 52% ahead of target and this year the total will be double that. "We have a weekly stand up review in each area. We ask if we have done what we said we would do in the previous week, and what we are going to do in the next. We also ask what are the obstacles to delivery. I attend virtually every review. It lets people know in only 10 to 15 minutes what we are going to do, the reason for doing it, its importance and what the benefits are to the business". The Operations Manager recall.

He carried on by saying "The benefits of good TPM spin out into so many areas. For example, We saw a direct correlation between reactive maintenance and accidents. If you are in breakdown mode, you are under pressure for production and you are trying to fix things fast. If you improve your breakdowns and unplanned failures, you will reduce your accidents. We reduced total accidents for the site from 35 in 2012 to five last year and lost time accidents have gone down from 12 to one. It's not just TPM it's changing the mindset to accept that things are their responsibility and no one else's and then challenging them to make a difference".

Over three years, the company made 35-40% OEE improvement in previously bottlenecked areas, directly contributing to bottom-line growth. We are totally convinced that the main driver is employee engagement coupled to clear performance measurement. One could ask; how hard is it to create that sense of involvement? It doesn't happen overnight, some are keen but the significant mass will wait to see which way it goes. It takes a lot of drive and focus and talking the same story over and over again. Every quarter the Operations Manager get out on his soapbox and give the talk and he is consistent; he is out on the shop floor constantly finding out if the team are doing what they say they are going to do and keeping focus on the things that really matter.

Chapter 24: Conclusion

As we mentioned in the earlier chapters of this book. Total Productive maintenance was developed by Japanese companies in response to what was then total quality control (TQC), they found that certain aspects of TQC (or TQM as we now know it) did not fit very well into a maintenance program. They therefore adapted the TQM around the various maintenance programs that they had seen in American firms such as Preventive maintenance and predictive maintenance and developed what we now know as TPM.

TPM holds the involvement of everyone as one of its key principles and thus makes the operators who use the machines more responsible for the upkeep of the machines as well as the running of them.

Obviously to get to this point the operators require training and many machines need improvement and modification to make them easy to clean and maintain, we therefore need a methodical implementation program to introduce them to TPM and autonomous maintenance.

This program is most commonly broken down into seven steps.

1. Cleaning and Inspecting

This is a similar stage to the 5S Shine stage with a similar purpose. We need to remove all dirt and grime from the machine, not for the purposes of making the machine pretty but to uncover and highlight any and all problems within the machine. This will require the machine to be taken out of production, all fluids drained and covers removed so that every part of the machine can be inspected and cleaned. We seek to remove the grime of past years and bring the machine back to how it was when it was first purchased, thoroughly inspecting each and every part of the machine to highlight any damage or wear.

We use Red Tags to highlight any problems, these problems if possible should be rectified immediately but if necessary a plan should be put in place to fix problems and remove the remaining red tags.

The cleaning and inspection should be done by the operators and maintenance crew responsible for the machine so that they become familiar with the machines details and can see where dirt accumulates and how and what problems are occurring.

2. Remove Causes of Contamination and improve Access

When we clean and inspect our machines we should look at where the dirt that we remove is coming from; is it being produced inside the machine or is it coming into the machine from outside. We should seek to either remove or minimise these sources of contamination that cause us to need to clean our machines.

We should also look at any areas that are difficult to reach or that may be unsafe to improve access to them so that future cleaning and inspection can be done without problems and as quickly as possible. This can also include the replacement of covers with Perspex or similar see through materials so that checking is much easier.

3. Cleaning and Lubrication Standards

The first two stages set the stage for the operators to define the maintenance steps that they can conduct to prevent further deterioration of the machine. They have to define what they will clean, lubricate, tighten and inspect, how they will do it, how often and so forth to ensure that they keep the machine in its optimum condition.

4. Train for general Inspections

We now have the experts (maintenance technicians, team leaders) conduct in depth training with the operators to explain the function and purpose of each component of the machine as well as training in problem solving skills such as the 5 whys; we then have the operators re-inspect the machines with their new-found knowledge and highlight any new problems discovered in much the same way that we did in stage one.

5. Conduct Autonomous Inspections

With what they have learned in stage 4 the operators modify the standards and instructions that they put in place for the first three stages of autonomous maintenance to streamline and improve their maintenance tasks.

The tasks at this stage are also compared and rationalized with the maintenance departments own maintenance schedules allowing tasks to be allocated correctly and prevent duplication of effort.

6. Implement Visual Maintenance Management

Just as in 5S, one of the main aims of TPM is standardisation, we seek to standardise the maintenance work that we do and also try to make the workplace as "visual" as possible. We create formal standards for our autonomous maintenance and look at improving the visual management of our machines. We highlight the direction of flow of fluids through pipe work, which way levers and valves have to be turned to open and close, highlight "safe" or "normal" operating values on gauges and sight glasses in green and undesirable readings in red, all to make things as obvious as possible to anyone if things are operating correctly. The various principles of 5S should be thoroughly applied not just to the machine but the relevant associated equipment, tools and materials.

A useful tool to use to visually monitor the maintenance process and 5S tasks is that of the Kamishabi board, this is a simple T card planning board that is placed in the work cell showing the various tasks that need to be completed each and every day and when. These cards should carry the instructions as to what needs to be done and when completed they should be turned on the board to reveal a different colour to show that they have been completed. The kamishabi board therefore provides a very quick and easy check for everyone in the organisation to see if tasks have been completed when they should have been.

7. Continuous Improvement

We repeat and improve on all that we have found and done in the previous stages to continually improve and reinforce what we are doing with autonomous maintenance. We maintain good records of what we have done and the failures that occur and so forth that can then be fed back to the maintenance technicians to be integrated into future designs of machines to improve reliability and make maintenance easier.

Team leaders, managers and maintenance technicians should also audit the work done by the operators on a regular basis to be able to both congratulate the operators on a job well done and to give them the benefits of their knowledge.